THE TERRORIST DIASPORA: AFTER THE FALL OF THE CALIPHATE

HEARING

BEFORE THE

TASK FORCE ON DENYING TERRORISTS ENTRY TO THE UNITED STATES

OF THE

COMMITTEE ON HOMELAND SECURITY HOUSE OF REPRESENTATIVES

ONE HUNDRED FIFTEENTH CONGRESS

FIRST SESSION

JULY 13, 2017

Serial No. 115–22

Printed for the use of the Committee on Homeland Security

Available via the World Wide Web: http://www.gpo.gov/fdsys/

U.S. GOVERNMENT PUBLISHING OFFICE

27–976 PDF   WASHINGTON : 2018

For sale by the Superintendent of Documents, U.S. Government Publishing Office
Internet: bookstore.gpo.gov   Phone: toll free (866) 512–1800; DC area (202) 512–1800
Fax: (202) 512–2104   Mail: Stop IDCC, Washington, DC 20402–0001

CONTENTS

Page

THE TERRORIST DIASPORA: AFTER THE FALL OF THE CALIPHATE

Thursday, July 13, 2017

U.S. HOUSE OF REPRESENTATIVES,
COMMITTEE ON HOMELAND SECURITY,
TASK FORCE ON DENYING TERRORISTS
ENTRY TO THE UNITED STATES,
Washington, DC.

The task force met, pursuant to notice, at 3:31 p.m., in Room HVC–210, Capitol Visitor Center, Hon. Mike Gallagher [Chairman of the task force] presiding.

Present: Representatives Gallagher, Higgins, Rutherford, Garrett, Fitzpatrick, Katko, Watson Coleman, Jackson Lee, and Barragán.

Mr. GALLAGHER. The Committee on Homeland Security Task Force on Denying Terrorists Entry into the United States will come to order. First of all, thank you all for being so patient.

Oftentimes you have to vote in Congress, and that can screw up our best-laid plans. So we really appreciate you sticking with us. This is an important topic, and we want to make sure we cover it as thoroughly as possible.

We are meeting today to examine the current terror threat landscape, how the terrorist diaspora will affect the security of the homeland, and what additional measures the United States can take to mitigate the threat.

In the interest of time, the Ranking Member and I have agreed to submit our opening statements for the record.

Without objection, so ordered. OK.

[The statements of Chairman Gallagher and Ranking Member Watson Coleman follow:]

STATEMENT OF CHAIRMAN MIKE GALLAGHER

JULY 13, 2017

Reports from the Middle East's conflict zones contain the positive news of U.S. and allied forces' successes in Syria and Iraq. In the past week, U.S.-backed forces in Syria have breached the wall around Raqqa's Old City, marking a major advance in the months-long battle to drive the Islamic State out of its self-declared capital. In Iraq this week, Prime Minister Abadi arrived in Mosul to formally declare victory after Iraqi troops fought back a fierce resistance from the Islamic State, literally fighting meter by meter, to gain control of the city.

Looming over news of victory are questions about the road ahead. Today, jihadi fighters are fleeing to other towns, concealing themselves among locals, and joining affiliates in places like Egypt, Libya, Yemen, Afghanistan, Nigeria, and the Philippines. A *New York Times* correspondent reported from Mosul that the recovered bodies of ISIS fighters are primarily from the Caucasus, leaving locals to believe that Iraqi fighters have been shaving their beards, blending into the population, and fleeing with groups of refugees. Nor is the fighting over. ISIS still retains much of Al Anbar Province in Iraq and the Euphrates River valley in Syria. When I left Al Anbar in 2008, the neighborhoods were safe enough to walk around without body armor. My unit and I were fortunate enough to hand out soccer balls and school supplies to Iraqi children who were starting school and finally living in a safer area and free from terror. Within 7 years, that province was under ISIS' control.

Western Europe, with its access to the United States, has been a particularly concerning source of foreign fighters. Secretary Kelly recently described as many as 10,000 European citizens that went to take part in the region's sectarian struggle. While many of those who went to fight are now dead, there are numerous fighters now seeking to return home. The *New York Times* reported that between 100 and 250 ideologically-driven foreigners are thought to have been smuggled into Europe between 2014 and mid-2016, nearly all through Turkey. These returning fighters pose a greater threat to the West than ever before. They have learned to make IEDs in many forms, deploy drones that can drop grenades, and engage in combat with a range of deadly weapons, including low-tech weaponry like vehicles. And they can use this knowledge to train a younger generation of Western citizens susceptible to radicalization.

Europe has had to bear the brunt of the so-called Caliphate's collapse. Facing the return of these jihadists, Europe has increased its defenses in many ways, including through increased intelligence collection and sharing, more programs to vet and screen travelers, and enhanced border security.

The question is whether these improvements are enough in light of today's grave threat. Authorities have not been able to identify all returnees, some of whom have sophisticated false documents. Patchwork screening and inconsistent border checks have allowed jihadists to hatch plots and hide from police by moving between European states. Additionally, limited intelligence sharing and unheeded warnings between the European Union's member states allows plotters to slip through the nets of law enforcement.

This task force's primary concern is the degree to which jihadists threaten the homeland. The United States also faces a threat from returning foreign fighters. Our Visa Waiver Program, which allows European citizens to travel to the United States without a visa and with less screening, does provide an opportunity for determined terrorists to exploit.

The United States and Europe's close relationship, based on a common history, shared values, and dependent economies, means that we must ensure the safety of travel across the Atlantic without disturbing tourist and commercial activity. The solution lies in our ability to quickly and effectively vet and screen travelers, gain sufficient intelligence from our allies, and act on credible threats when identified.

This task force was established to determine the threat that jihadists and returning foreign fighters pose to the homeland and our ability to meet that threat through the Department of Homeland Security's vetting and screening infrastructure.

I look forward to hearing from our expert witnesses on the current threat and commensurate U.S. defenses. I thank the witnesses for being here and for the research they are conducting at Foundation for Defense of Democracies, the Heritage Foundation, and the Rand Corporation, which has informed lawmakers and the Executive branch on this critical topic.

STATEMENT OF RANKING MEMBER BONNIE WATSON COLEMAN

JULY 13, 2017

Tens of thousands of foreign fighters from countries around the globe have traveled to Iraq and Syria to engage in the fight on behalf of ISIS. The vast majority of these individuals are thought to be from Europe, with a far smaller number coming from the United States. Over time, many of these fighters have begun to return home, raising concerns about the security threat they may pose both to their native countries and nations abroad.

On this task force, we are charged with examining the potential threat foreign fighters and other terrorists may pose to the United States in particular. Specifically, we are focused on how our Government can identify foreign fighters who may seek to travel to this country to do us harm and deny them entry.

This is no easy task, to be sure. Travel to and from the so-called caliphate is generally clandestine, and many countries lack either the capacity to collect information on their returning citizens or the will to share it with our Government.

Given this challenge, I strongly agree with the testimony of our witness, Dr. Clarke, that our first priority in addressing the foreign fighter threat should be detection. We must identify returning foreign fighters so we can determine which have the intent and means to travel to the United States to carry out an attack and focus our efforts to deny them entry to this country.

That, in turn, requires increasing information sharing with partner nations and enhancing their capacity to screen potential terrorists. This initiative must be done cooperatively, recognizing the sovereignty of other nations and their varying laws and technological capacity, while underscoring our shared interest in this important goal.

Unfortunately, I am concerned that the Trump administration's travel ban and rhetoric about Muslims as well as alienation of our friends in Europe is counterproductive to the kind of multilateral cooperation that is necessary. I hope we can overcome these unfortunate actions to work cooperatively in the interest of the security of America.

Today, I look forward to hearing the assessment of our witness panel about what our Government is currently doing to address the threat of returning foreign fighters to the homeland, and what more can and should be done.

Of course, addressing the potential threat posed by returning foreign fighters is just one part of securing the homeland. But as events continue to unfold in Syria and more fighters return home, coinciding with increased attacks in Europe, we must ensure we are doing all we can to secure our Nation from this threat.

I know the Members of this task force are deeply committed to doing our part in that effort, on a bipartisan basis, and I am pleased to be a part of it.

Mr. GALLAGHER. With that, we are lucky—and the other Members of the committee are reminded that their statements may be submitted for the record as well.

[The statements of Ranking Member Thompson and Honorable Jackson Lee follows:]

STATEMENT OF RANKING MEMBER BENNIE G. THOMPSON

JULY 13, 2017

This committee has a long history of addressing terrorist travel to the United States through its oversight and legislative work. Today's task force hearing will address a topic that has been addressed by a previous committee task force and subcommittees.

The rising number of foreign fighters returning from Iraq and Syria to Europe, along with increased terrorist attacks in Europe, raises concern about the possibility of foreign fighters from Europe or elsewhere seeking to enter this country to do us harm.

Identifying foreign fighters among the millions of legitimate travelers to the United States each year is a serious challenge for the Department of Homeland Security and other Federal agencies.

Individuals have become more sophisticated about traveling to the so-called caliphate undetected. Many of our foreign partners have limited ability to track their returnees and information sharing can be a challenge. It is therefore incumbent upon the United States to continue to enhance our capacity to identify those who have traveled to Iraq and Syria for terrorist purposes and support our partners' capacity to do the same.

It is also imperative that we strengthen information-sharing agreements and practices with foreign governments to ensure that they are providing information about their returnees who may pose a threat to the United States. This effort requires diplomacy and relationship building, neither of which have been a strong suit of the Trump administration thus far. Oftentimes, putting "America first" means working with foreign partners rather than alienating them.

I know the operators at DHS and other Federal agencies have forged good working relationships with their foreign counterparts. Perhaps the administration at its highest level could take a lesson from them.

I would also note that 7 months into the Trump presidency, the Department of Homeland Security still has numerous vacancies in critical leadership positions, including those integral to addressing the foreign fighter threat, including commissioner of Customs and Border Protection and director of Immigration and Customs Enforcement, under secretary for Intelligence and Analysis, and assistant secretary for the Office of Policy.

"Acting" agency heads may be career officials with substantial expertise, but they are generally not empowered to implement new policies and initiatives. The White House needs to ensure the Department has confirmed leadership in place to deal with emerging and evolving threats like the matter before the Task Force this afternoon.

———

STATEMENT OF HONORABLE SHEILA JACKSON LEE

JULY 13, 2017

Chairman Mike Gallagher and Ranking Member Bonnie Watson Coleman thank you for leading this task force as we consider the important question of "Denying Terrorists Entry to the United States: Examining Visa Security."

Today's hearing allows Members of the task force to examine the current status of the changes to the terror threat landscape as ISIS continues to lose ground in Syria and Iraq and foreign fighters begin to return to their home countries.

I look forward to exploring strategies and policy changes that are needed to combat this emerging threat, particularly as it relates to the homeland security.

I welcome today's witnesses:
- Mr. Thomas Joscelyn, senior fellow with the Foundation for Defense of Democracies;
- Mr. Robin Simcox, Margaret Thatcher fellow, with the Heritage Foundation; and
- Dr. Colin P. Clarke (Democratic witness), political scientist, with The RAND Corporation.

The task force will examine all pathways by which extremists might infiltrate the homeland and will seek to identify gaps in U.S. Government information-sharing and vetting procedures.

As for those of us who are senior Members of this committee, we understand how important it is to protect the security of our homeland from those who would do it harm.

The purpose of the hearing is to examine the current status of the changes to the terror threat landscape as ISIS continues to lose ground in Syria and Iraq and foreign fighters begin to return to their home countries. Members of the task force will also explore strategies and policy changes that are needed to combat this emerging threat, particularly as it relates to the homeland. This is also an opportunity for the task force to exam how the U.S. Government can address foreign fighters who may seek to enter this country.

Last Congress, I introduced H.R. 48, the "No Fly For Foreign Fighters Act." This legislation sought to help keep foreign fighters and terrorists from entering our country through an American airport.

Specifically, the "No Fly for Foreign Fighters Act" required the director of the Terrorist Screening Center to review the completeness of the Terrorist Screening Database and the terrorist watch list utilized by the Transportation Security Administration to determine if an individual who may seek to board a U.S.-bound or domestic flight, and who poses a threat to aviation or national security or a threat of terrorism and is known or suspected of being a member of a foreign terrorist organization, is included in the database and on such watch list.

The route that the terrorist used on September 11, 2001 was commercial aircraft that they turned into improvised explosives that killed over 3,000 people, and caused life-changing injuries to hundreds of others.

The efforts to combat terrorism that began as a result of this attack.

As of December 2015, during ISIS' peak, up to 31,000 people from 86 countries had traveled to Iraq and Syria to fight with ISIS and other extremist groups.

Today, due to the determination and focus of the United States and our allies, which include predominantly Muslim nations in the region, cooperative intelligence assessments have limited the number of foreign fighter recruits entering Syria to as few as 50 per month.

It is unclear when or if there will ever be an articulable "fall" of the "caliphate" or ending of ISIS, but it is clear that there has been and will continue to be a disbanding and subsequent reduction in its influence and ability to operate as a terrorist group.

The lessons we have learned over the past 15 years is that we need cooperation and collaboration from Muslim nations to win the war on terrorism.

This is why the Executive Order issued by the President banning Muslims from predominately Muslim countries from entering the United States was so problematic to the our National interest in combating terrorism.

The action has been:
(1) denounced by leading National security and foreign policy experts,
(2) deemed unconstitutional by scores of law professors and other scholars,
(3) sparked peaceful mass demonstrations across the Nation, and
(4) opposed by a majority of the American public, and enjoined by at least five Federal district courts before the Supreme Court ruled.

The court is allowing the ban to go into effect for foreign nationals who lack any "bona fide relationship with any person or entity in the United States."

The court's unsigned opinion protects the vast majority of people seeking to enter the United States to visit a relative, accept a job, attend a university, or deliver a speech.

The court said the ban could not be imposed on anyone who had "a credible claim of a bona fide relationship with a person or entity in the United States."

What the travel ban did was despoil our relations with these six countries, and much of the Muslim world, which sees the ban, rightly, as religiously-motivated.

It also diminishes our stature in the eyes of our allies who are taking in tens of thousands of refugees without excuses or complaint.

So instead of strengthening relations with countries that should be our allies and partners in the fight against terrorism, we alienate them, inflame sentiment against the United States among their citizens, and deprive ourselves of vital intelligence and resources needed to fight the root causes of terror.

According to the Pew Center, about 3 million refugees have been resettled in the United States since Congress passed the Refugee Act of 1980, which created the Federal Refugee Resettlement Program and the current National standard for the screening and admission of refugees into the country.

California, Texas, and New York resettled nearly a quarter of all refugees in fiscal 2016, together taking 20,738 refugees. Other States that received at least 3,000 refugees included Michigan, Ohio, Arizona, North Carolina, Washington, Pennsylvania, and Illinois. By contrast, Arkansas, the District of Columbia, and Wyoming each resettled fewer than 10 refugees. Delaware and Hawaii took in no refugees.

It is deeply disturbing to me that the President's nominee to be the next Attorney General, Sen. Jeff Sessions of Alabama, appears not be troubled in the slightest by cavalier rejection of the principle of religious liberty implicit in the Executive Order.

The Committee on Homeland Security is committed to ensure that no terrorists will have the opportunity to do such great harm to neither the United States nor its people ever again.

I thank the Members of the task force who will work toward a better understanding of the threats posed by terrorist and how this committee and Nation may better prepare to repel them.

I am looking forward to hearing what our witnesses have to say and I am sure they have important testimony.

Mr. GALLAGHER. We are very pleased to welcome a distinguished panel of witnesses before us today on this very, very important topic.

Mr. Thomas Joscelyn, a senior fellow at the Foundation for Defense of Democracies, Mr. Robin Simcox, the Margaret Thatcher fellow at the Heritage Foundation, and Dr. Colin P. Clarke, political scientist at the RAND Corporation. Thank you for being here today. The witnesses' full written statements will appear in the record.

The Chair now recognizes Mr. Joscelyn for 5 minutes for an opening statement.

STATEMENT OF THOMAS JOSCELYN, SENIOR FELLOW, FOUNDATION FOR DEFENSE OF DEMOCRACIES

Mr. JOSCELYN. Well, thank you, Chairman Gallagher and Ranking Member Watson Coleman for having me here today. I appreciate it—and Members of the committee.

Mr. GALLAGHER. Did you turn it on?

Mr. JOSCELYN. I turned it on, yes. What is wrong? I am all right. Thank you.

So just in brief, I will try and keep this very quick. You know, there is a lot of talk now with ISIS losing Mosul and the push into Raqqa about its impending defeat. I am here to sort-of basically blow a horn of caution on that.

I think that ISIS is a very resilient organization. We have seen them come back from defeats in the past. I would say, if you look at my written testimony, there are some points in there I would make very quickly.

I don't even know that we know how many fighters they have left to this day. You know, this is the type of metric which is very simple to ask and yet you look back through the U.S. Government's pronouncements in terms of ISIS, where at the beginning of the air campaign the CIA estimated they had 20,000 to 30,000 fighters, approximately. U.S. military now says we have killed about 70,000 fighters since September 2014.

So if you go by those metrics it, you know, it looks like the U.S. Government is saying that we basically killed more than two times the upper-end estimate of what this organization had at the beginning of the air campaign. I think that that speaks.

The lesson I draw from that is that probably we do not know how many total fighters they have and that with all these sort-of, you know, pronouncements that we are seeing about their defeat in Mosul and pending defeat in Raqqa, be very careful because they have enough personnel left to wage insurgency in the near future and on-going.

They are experts at guerilla warfare. They have known this is coming. This is not something that they are going to disappear overnight at all.

Second point is that they are now an international organization. In November 2014, Abu Bakr al Baghdadi announced that his organization now had so-called provinces around the world.

Some of these, as I say in my written testimony, amounted to nothing more than just small terror cells. Others metastasized or grew into full-scale insurgencies themselves, whether they be in Libya where they temporarily captured the city of Sirte or as we have seen in the Sinai and a few other hotspots.

So what that means from a terrorist travel perspective is there is a lot of focus on Syria and Iraq, but this is not an organization that is only located in Syria and Iraq.

That their membership and their leadership is actually dispersed and that they have what is known by the U.S. military and U.S. intelligence as external attack planners that are outside of Iraq and Syria who are capable of planning attacks against the West, including in Libya where some of those plots have been detected.

Another quick point on this is that you will see in my written testimony that there was a recent report put out by Europol which I think had some very fascinating statistics in it.

That report sort-of highlighted for me the fact that while the returnees are an issue from Iraq and Syria and elsewhere into Europe and potentially through Europe to here, although that is very difficult for them to pull off.

Although the returnees are an issue from these war zones, that actually most of the arrests that take place in Europe today are actually of people who were either citizens or residents already of European nations.

So for example, they listed in that report that in 2015 there were 41 arrests of returnees from Iraq and Syria. In 2016 there were 22. The total number of arrests in 2015 for jihadi terrorism-related incidents or suspected incidents, was 687 and in 2016 it was 718.

In other words, this leads to my next point, the problem when it comes to terrorist travel is not just about returnees coming back from the battlefields, but we have now, unfortunately, a situation where citizens and residents of European nations, according to European statistics, are by far the more numerous potential threats.

For travel here that raises the issue of a citizen in the United Kingdom or France or somewhere where it is easier for them to get on a plane and get here to potentially do damage.

Finally, and I will just wrap up, every one of these hearings I always sort-of always mention al-Qaeda. You already had another hearing on al-Qaeda today so I won't belabor the point, but al-Qaeda is still very much alive.

There was a recent plot that was actually announced by the Department of Justice on June 29, which I think is very important to keep in mind. They announced that after 2 years they actually announced this plea deal that this guy entered into who was from Ohio.

He actually had gone off to Syria where he trained for a few months and came back. He was sent back here by senior al-Qaeda operatives in 2014 to establish a cell to launch an attack here in the United States.

This was under the radar. As a counterterrorism nerd who studies this stuff very closely, we didn't know about this for, you know, a couple years. The Department of Justice announced this on June 29.

To me, it is a lone case. It is an isolated case, but it emphasizes the fact that you are not just dealing with ISIS returnees or ISIS fighters who are coming abroad and who want to come back and do harm. You also still have to worry about al-Qaeda. We can talk more about that.

[The prepared statement of Mr. Joscelyn follows:]

PREPARED STATEMENT OF THOMAS JOSCELYN

JULY 13, 2017

Chairman Gallagher, Ranking Member Watson Coleman, and other distinguished committee Members, thank you for inviting me to testify today concerning foreign fighters and the threat some of them pose to the United States and Europe.

The fall of Mosul and the likely fall of Raqqa won't be the end of the Islamic State. The group has already reverted to its insurgent roots in some of the areas that have been lost. It also still controls some territory. The Islamic State will continue to function as a guerrilla army, despite suffering significant losses. In May, the Office of the Director of National Intelligence (ODNI) assessed that even though it was losing significant ground, the Islamic State "will likely have enough resources and fighters to sustain insurgency operations and plan terrorists [sic] attacks in the region and internationally" going forward.[1] Unfortunately, I think ODNI's assess-

---

[1] Daniel R. Coats, Director of National Intelligence, Statement for the Record, "Worldwide Threat Assessment of the U.S. Intelligence Community," Senate Select Committee on Intelligence, May 11, 2017, p. 21 (*https://www.intelligence.senate.gov/sites/default/files/documents/os-coats-051117.pdf*).

ment is accurate for a number of reasons, some of which I outline below. I also discuss some hypothetical scenarios, especially with respect to returning foreign fighters or other supporters already living in Europe or the United States.

Recent history.—The Islamic State's predecessor quickly recovered from its losses during the American-led "surge," capitalizing on the war in Syria and a politically poisonous environment in Iraq to rebound. Indeed, Abu Bakr al Baghdadi's organization grew into an international phenomenon by the end of 2014, just 3 years after the U.S. withdrawal from Iraq was completed. Baghdadi's men did this while defying al-Qaeda's leaders and competing with rival jihadist groups. This recent history should give us pause any time we hear rhetoric that sounds too optimistic about the end of the Islamic State's caliphate. The enterprise has had enough resources at its disposal to challenge multiple actors for more than 3 years. There is no question that the Islamic State's finances, senior personnel, and other assets have been hit hard. But it is premature to say its losses amount to a deathblow.

Uncertainty regarding size of total membership.—While it is no longer at the peak of its power, the Islamic State likely still has thousands of dedicated members. We don't even really know how many members it has in Iraq and Syria, let alone around the globe. Previous U.S. estimates almost certainly undercounted the group's ranks. In September 2014, at the beginning of the U.S.-led air campaign, the CIA reportedly estimated that the Islamic State could "muster" between 20,000 and 31,500 fighters.[2] This figure was "more than three times the previous estimates," CNN noted.[3] By December 2016, the U.S. military was estimating that 50,000 Islamic State fighters had been killed.[4] By February 2017, U.S. Special Operations command concluded that more than 60,000 jihadists had perished.[5] Two months later, in April 2017, the Pentagon reportedly estimated that 70,000 Islamic State fighters had been killed.[6]

Taken at face value, these figures (beginning with the September 2014 approximation) would suggest that Abu Bakr al Baghdadi's enterprise was able to replace its entire force structure more than two times over, while fighting multiple enemies on numerous fronts. This is, of course, highly unlikely. Even with its prolific recruiting campaign, it would be impossible for any cohesive fighting organization, let alone one under the sustained pressure faced by the Islamic State, to train, equip and deploy fighters this quickly. It is far more likely that the United States never had a good handle on how many jihadists are in its ranks and the casualty figures are guesstimates. The purpose of citing these figures is not to re-litigate the past, but instead to sound a cautionary alarm regarding the near-future: We likely do not even know how many members the Islamic State has in Iraq and Syria today.

The Islamic State is an international organization.—Since November 2014, when Abu Bakr al Baghdadi first announced the establishment of "provinces" around the globe, the Islamic State's membership grew outside of Iraq and Syria. This further complicates any effort to estimate its overall size. Some of these "provinces" were nothing more than small terror networks, while others evolved into capable insurgency organizations in their own right. The Libyan branch of the caliphate temporarily controlled the city of Sirte. Although the jihadists were ejected from their Mediterranean abode by the end of 2016, they still have some forces inside the country. Similarly, Wilayah Khorasan (or Khorasan province), which represents the "caliphate" in Afghanistan and Pakistan, seized upwards of ten districts in Afghanistan as of early 2016, but has since lost ground. More recently, jihadists in the Philippines seized much of Marawi, hoisting the Islamic State's black banner over the city. Wilayah Sinai controls at least some turf, and is able to launch spectacular attacks on security forces. It was responsible for downing a Russian airliner in October 2015. Other "provinces" exist in East Africa, West Africa, Yemen, and elsewhere.

---

[2] Jim Sciutto, Jamie Crawford and Chelsea J. Carter, "ISIS can 'muster' between 20,000 and 31,500 fighters, CIA says," CNN.com, September 12, 2014 (*http://www.cnn.com/2014/09/11/world/meast/isis-syria-iraq/index.html*).

[3] Ibid.

[4] *Reuters*, "U.S. estimates 50,000 Islamic State fighters killed so far: U.S. official," December 8, 2016. (*http://mobile.reuters.com/article/worldNews/idUSKBN13X28N*) See also: Ryan Browne, "US Special Ops chief: More than 60,000 ISIS fighters killed," CNN.com, February 15, 2017 (*http://www.cnn.com/2017/02/14/politics/isis-60000-fighters-killed/index.html*).

[5] Ryan Browne, "US Special Ops chief: More than 60,000 ISIS fighters killed," CNN.com, February 15, 2017 (*http://www.cnn.com/2017/02/14/politics/isis-60000-fighters-killed/index.html*).

[6] Molly Hennessy-Fiske and W.J. Hennigan, "Civilian casualties from airstrikes grow in Iraq and Syria. But few are ever investigated," *Los Angeles Times*, April 21, 2017 (*http://www.latimes.com/projects/la-fg-iraq-airstrikes/*).

In May, the Office of the Director of National Intelligence (ODNI) reported that the so-called caliphate "is seeking to foster interconnectedness among its global branches and networks, align their efforts to ISIS's strategy, and withstand counter-ISIS efforts."[7] Gen. John Nicholson, the commander of U.S. Forces-Afghanistan, has said that Wilayah Khorasan went through an "application process" and the Islamic State mothership provided it with "advice," "publicity," and "some financial support."[8] Although it is impossible to judge the extent of the Islamic State's cohesion, as much of the data is not available, there is at least some connectivity between the group's leadership and its "provinces" elsewhere. This is best seen on the media side, as the organization is particularly adept at disseminating messages from around the globe in multiple languages, despite some recent hiccups in this regard.

While their fortunes may rise or fall at any given time, this global network of Islamic State "provinces" will remain a formidable problem for the foreseeable future. Not only are they capable of killing large numbers of people in the countries they operate in, this structure also makes tracking international terrorist travel more difficult. For instance, counterterrorism officials have tied plots in Europe to operatives in Libya.[9] This indicates that some of the Islamic State's "external plotters," who are responsible for targeting the West, are not stationed in Iraq and Syria. The U.S.-led air campaign has disrupted the Islamic State's "external operations" capacity by killing a number of jihadists in this wing of the organization. But others live.

The cult of martyrdom has grown.—A disturbingly large number of people are willing to kill themselves for the Islamic State's cause. The number of suicide bombings claimed by the so-called caliphate dwarfs all other jihadist groups, including al-Qaeda. In 2016, for instance, the Islamic State claimed 1,112 "martyrdom operations" in Iraq and Syria alone.[10] Through the first 6 months of 2017, the organization claimed another 527 such bombings (nearly three-fourths of them using vehicle-borne improvised explosive devices, or VBIEDs) in those two countries. These figures do not include suicide attacks in other nations where Abu Bakr al Baghdadi's loyalists are known to operate.

To put the Islamic State's current "martyrdom operations" in perspective, consider data published by the *Washington Post* in 2008.[11] According to the *Post,* there were just 54 suicide attacks in all of 2001, when al-Qaeda's "martyrs" launched the most devastating terrorist airline hijackings in history. The Islamic State currently eclipses that figure every month in Iraq and Syria, averaging 93 suicide bombings per month in 2016 and 88 per month so far in 2017. Many of these operations are carried out by foreign fighters.

These suicide bombers have been mainly used to defend Islamic State positions, including the city of Mosul, which was one of the self-declared caliphate's two capitals. For instance, half of the "martyrdom operations" carried out in Iraq and Syria this year (265 of the 527 claimed) took place in Nineveh province, which is home to Mosul. The "martyrs" were dispatched with increasing frequency after the campaign to retake the city began in October 2016, with 501 claimed suicide bombings in and around Mosul between then and the end of June 2017.

Some caveats are in order. It is impossible to verify the Islamic State's figures with any precision. The fog of war makes all reporting spotty and not every suicide bombing attempt is recorded in published accounts. Some of the claimed "martyrdom operations" likely failed to hit their targets, but were counted by the Islamic State as attacks anyway. The U.S.-led coalition and Iraqi forces have routinely taken out VBIEDs before drivers could reach their mark. Not all "martyrs" are truly willing recruits. For instance, the Islamic State's figures include numerous children who were pressed into service by Baghdadi's goons.

---

[7] Daniel R. Coats, Director of National Intelligence, Statement for the Record, "Worldwide Threat Assessment of the U.S. Intelligence Community," Senate Select Committee on Intelligence, May 11, 2017, p. 5 (*https://www.intelligence.senate.gov/sites/default/files/documents/os-coats-051117.pdf*).

[8] Department of Defense Press Briefing by General Nicholson in the Pentagon Briefing Room, December 2, 2016 (*https://www.defense.gov/News/Transcripts/Transcript-View/Article/1019029/department-of-defense-press-briefing-by-general-nicholson-in-the-pentagon-brief/*).

[9] Thomas Joscelyn, "Pentagon: Bombs struck Islamic State's 'external plotters' in Libya," *FDD's Long War Journal,* January 21, 2017 (*http://www.longwarjournal.org/archives/2017/01/pentagon-bombs-struck-islamic-states-external-plotters-in-libya.php*).

[10] All of the figures cited in this section are derived from infographics produced by the Islamic State's Amaq News Agency. As discussed, there are some important caveats to keep in mind when evaluating these statistics.

[11] *Washingtonpost.com,* "Suicide Attacks Increase and Spread." (*http://www.washingtonpost.com/wp-dyn/content/graphic/2008/04/18/GR2008041800293.html?sid=-ST2008041800913*).

Still, even taking into account these caveats, it is reasonable to conclude that the number of people willing to die for the sake of the so-called caliphate is disturbingly high—much higher than the number of willing martyrs in 2001 or even much more recently. Even though most of these people have been deployed in war zones, it is possible that more will be used outside of Iraq and Syria if they survive the fight and are able to travel to other countries. The Islamic State has already had some success in instigating would-be recruits to die for its cause in the West after they failed to emigrate to the lands of the caliphate. It is certainly possible that more will be sent into Europe or the United States in the future.

Children used in suicide attacks, executions, and other operations.—The Islamic State has a robust program, named "Cubs of the Caliphate," for indoctrinating children. It is one of the most disturbing aspects of the organization's operations. Not only does the Islamic State's propaganda frequently feature children attending classes, its videos have proudly displayed the jihadists' use of children as executioners.

Earlier this month, for instance, the group's Wilayah Jazirah disseminated a video entitled, "They Left Their Beds Empty." Four children are shown beheading Islamic State captives. The same production is laced with footage of the terrorists responsible for the November 2015 Paris attacks, as well as other plots in Europe. Indeed, the children are made to reenact some of the same execution scenes that the Paris attackers carried out before being deployed. The Islamic State's message is clear: A new generation of jihadists is being raised to replace those who have fallen, including those who have already struck inside Europe.

The "Cubs of the Caliphate" program is not confined to Iraq and Syria, but also operates in Afghanistan and elsewhere. This means that numerous children who have been indoctrinated in the Islamic State's ways will pose a disturbing challenge for authorities going forward. As I noted above, some have already been used in "martyrdom operations" in Iraq and Syria. It is possible that others could be used in a similar fashion outside of the group's battlefields, in Europe or the United States. One purpose behind making children or adults commit heinous acts is to shock their conscience into thinking there is no way back, that they have crossed a threshold and there is no return. There are no easy answers for how to best deal with this problem.

Diversity of terrorist plots.—There are legitimate concerns about the possibility of well-trained fighters leaving Iraq and Syria for the West now that the Islamic State is losing its grip on some of its most important locales. We saw the damage that a team of Islamic State operatives can do in November 2015, when multiple locations in Paris were assaulted. Trained operatives have had a hand in other plots as well. This concern was succinctly expressed by EUROPOL in a recent report. "The number of returnees is expected to rise, if IS [Islamic State], as seems likely, is defeated militarily or collapses. An increasing number of returnees will likely strengthen domestic jihadist movements and consequently magnify the threat they pose to the EU."[12] While a true military defeat will be elusive, the central point stated here has merit, even though the number of arrests of returnees across Europe has recently declined. According to EUROPOL, "[a]rrests for traveling to conflict zones for terrorist purposes . . . decreased: From 141 in 2015 to 177 in 2016." And there was a similar "decrease in numbers of arrests of people returning from the conflict zones in Syria and Iraq: From 41 in 2015 to 22 in 2016."[13]

However, the overall number of arrests "related to jihadist terrorism" rose from 687 in 2015 to 718 in 2015, meaning that most of these terror-related arrests do not involve returnees.[14]

Still, returnees and the logistical support networks that facilitate travel to Iraq and Syria were prominently represented in court cases tried by EUROPOL member states. "As evidenced in the past couple of years, the majority of the verdicts for jihadist terrorism concerned offences related to the conflict in Syria and Iraq," EUROPOL reported in its statistical review for 2016. "They involved persons who had prepared to leave for or have returned from the conflict zone, as well as persons who have recruited, indoctrinated, financed or facilitated others to travel to Syria and/or Iraq to join the terrorist groups fighting there." In addition, "[i]ndividuals

---

[12] EUROPOL, "EU Terrorism Situation and Trend Report 2017," p. 7 (*https://www.europol.europa.eu/activities-services/main-reports/eu-terrorism-situation-and-trend-report-te-sat–2017*).

[13] EUROPOL, "EU Terrorism Situation and Trend Report 2017," p. 10 (*https://www.europol.europa.eu/activities-services/main-reports/eu-terrorism-situation-and-trend-report-te-sat–2017*).

[14] Ibid.

and cells preparing attacks in Europe and beyond were also brought before courts."[15]

These data show that while the threat posed by returnees is real, it is just one part of the overall threat picture. The Islamic State has encouraged supporters in the West to lash out in their home countries instead of traveling abroad, directed plots via "remote-control" guides, and otherwise inspired individuals to act on their own. These tactics often don't require professional terrorists to be dispatched from abroad. The Islamic State has also lowered the bar for what is considered a successful attack, amplifying concepts first espoused by others, especially al-Qaeda. A crude knife or machete attack that kills few people is trumpeted as the work of an Islamic State "soldier" or "fighter." On Bastille Day in Nice, France last year, an Islamic State supporter killed more than 80 people simply by running them over with a lorry. Other Islamic State supporters have utilized this simple technique, repeatedly advocated by Abu Bakr al Baghdadi's propagandists, as well.

However, I would urge caution. While the amateurs or individual actors have become more lethal over time, the risk of professionally-trained jihadists carrying out a mass casualty attack remains distinct. On average, the professionals can still do more damage than their amateur counterparts—if they are not stopped before-hand. The threat to aviation demonstrates the point. In October 2015, the Islamic State's Wilayah Sinai downed a Russian airliner, killing all 224 people on board. Although the jihadists claim to have used a crude improvised explosive device, the plot required that well-placed personnel implant it at an optimal location within the aircraft. U.S. officials are attempting to stop even more sophisticated devices, built by either the Islamic State or al-Qaeda, from being placed on-board flights bound for Europe or America. Other professionally-planned attacks could involve bombing commuter trains, Mumbai-style sieges, or multi-pronged assaults. Therefore, if the professionals are able to evade security measures, they could easily kill more people than the average amateur.

Counterterrorism services in Europe and the United States have stopped a number of professional plots through the years. Some of those foiled in the past year may have been more serious than realized at the time. However, there is a risk that as counterterrorism authorities deal with a large number of individual or amateur plots, the professional terrorists will be able to find another window of opportunity. The various threats posed by the Islamic State have placed great strains on our defenses.

The Islamic State could seek to exploit refugee flows once again. "The influx of refugees and migrants to Europe from existing and new conflict zones is expected to continue," EUROPOL reported in its review of 2016. The Islamic State "has already exploited the flow of refugees and migrants to send individuals to Europe to commit acts of terrorism, which became evident in the 2015 Paris attacks." The so-called caliphate and "possibly other jihadist terrorist organizations may continue to do so."[16] While the overwhelming majority of migrants are seeking to better their lives, some will continue to pose a terrorist threat. European nations are dealing with this, in part, by deploying more "investigators" to "migration hotspots in Greece and soon also to Italy."[17] These "guest officers" will rotate "at key points on the external borders of the European Union to strengthen security checks on the inward flows of migrants, in order to identify suspected terrorists and criminals, establishing a second line of defense."[18]

This makes it imperative that U.S. authorities share intelligence with their European counterparts and receive information in return to better track potential threats. The United States has led efforts to disrupt the Islamic State's "external attack" arm and probably has the best intelligence available on its activities. But European nations have vital intelligence as well, and only by combining data can officials get a better sense of the overall picture. Recent setbacks with respect to this intelligence sharing, after details of British investigations were leaked in the American press, are troubling. But we can hope that these relationships have been repaired, or will be soon.

It should be noted that would-be jihadists who are already citizens of European countries could have an easier route into the United States than migrants fleeing the battlefields. It is much easier for a British citizen to get on a plane headed for the United States than for an Islamic State operative posing as a Syrian refugee to enter the United States clandestinely through Europe. Given recent events in the United Kingdom, and the overall scale of the jihadist threat inside Britain, this

---

[15] EUROPOL, "EU Terrorism Situation and Trend Report 2017," p. 18.
[16] EUROPOL, "EU Terrorism Situation and Trend Report 2017," p. 6.
[17] EUROPOL, "EU Terrorism Situation and Trend Report 2017," p. 61.
[18] Ibid.

makes intelligence sharing on potential terrorists all the more crucial. British officials have said that they are investigating 500 possible plots involving 3,000 people on the "top list" of suspects at any given time. In addition, 20,000 people have been on the counterterrorism radar for one reason or another and are still considered potentially problematic.[19]

Exporting terror know-how.—It is possible that more of the Islamic State's terrorist inventions will be exported from abroad into Europe or the United States. As the self-declared caliphate sought to defend its lands, it devised all sorts of new means for waging war. It modified drones with small explosives and built its own small arms, rockets, bombs, and the like. Al-Qaeda first started to publish ideas for backpack bombs and other IEDs in its on-line manuals. The Islamic State has done this as well, but we shouldn't be surprised if some of its other inventions migrate out of the war zones. The group could do this by publishing technical details in its propaganda, or in-person, with experienced operatives carrying this knowledge with them.

Mr. GALLAGHER. Thank you, Mr. Joscelyn.

The Chair now recognizes Mr. Simcox for 5 minutes for an opening statement.

STATEMENT OF ROBIN SIMCOX, MARGARET THATCHER FELLOW, THE HERITAGE FOUNDATION

Mr. SIMCOX. Chairman Gallagher, distinguished Members of the committee, thank you for the opportunity to testify here today. The views I express during this testimony are my own and do not represent the official position of the Heritage Foundation.

My goal this afternoon is to highlight the ways in which foreign fighters returning from Syria and Iraq pose a clear risk to the West. I will focus particularly on the European components of this phenomenon.

There are three aspects to the threat which I will discuss today: The short term, the medium term and the long term. In the short term, at least 5,000 to 6,000 Europeans have fought alongside ISIS, al-Qaeda, and other Islamist groups in Syria and Iraq.

Some have already been killed in the fighting, and as ISIS' caliphate in Iraq and Syria comes under more pressure, yet more will be. However, there is also an expectation that many foreign fighters will disperse and inevitably some of these individuals are going to return to their home countries.

There could be approximately 1,000 returnees just from the United Kingdom, France, and Germany. The risk posed by these returning fighters is clear. Members of the cell that committed ISIS' attacks in Paris in November 2015, killing 130 and wounding 368, had traveled to Syria from Europe, fought and trained with ISIS, and then returned to Europe to carry out an attack.

This cell also contained ISIS members who had entered Europe from Syria after making false asylum claims. Those plugged into the same network then committed the attacks in Brussels in March 2016.

It is worth noting that American citizens were killed in both the Paris and Brussels attacks. Clearly the threat is not consigned solely to the homeland.

In the medium term, even if these returning fighters do not immediately plan to carry out terrorist attacks in the West, that does not mean they are still not detrimental to National security. In the

---

[19] BBC, "General election 2017: Extremist exclusion orders 'used'," May 28, 2017 (*http://www.bbc.com/news/election-2017-40072251*).

United Kingdom—these fighters will not be returning into a vacuum. They will be reconnecting with pre-existing Islamist networks.

The United Kingdom, for example, has approximately 23,000 terror suspects on the intelligence radar. Those who fought in previous foreign conflicts, such as Afghanistan in the 1980's and Bosnia in the 1990's earned gravitas and credibility as heroic returning members of the Mujahedeen. This helped propel a younger generation toward radicalism.

Take the example of a British citizen, Babar Ahmad. Ahmad, who pleaded guilty to terrorism offenses in the United States in 2013 fought in Bosnia in the 1990's and then returned to London.

True he did not commit a terrorist attack there; however, he was able to leverage his experience fighting in Bosnia to become one of the key radicalizers in the entire country upon return. He inspired a younger generation of radicals to take up the fight.

Moving on to the long term, entire families from the West move to Syria to live in this caliphate. Furthermore, there have been children born in Syria to Western parents.

So it is not just adults now returning to Europe. It is also their children. These children will have at minimum been hugely exposed to ISIS' ideology and most likely been indoctrinated with it.

There are almost 500 children currently in Syria with connections to France. There are approximately 80 Dutch children born in the caliphate and as many as 50 from the United Kingdom.

Europol has warned that ISIS will likely, "train these minors to become the next generation of foreign terrorist fighters." Knowing how to deal with the potential security threat posed by children of hardened ISIS fighters is a major long-term problem for Western governments.

Furthermore, there is already a clear problem on this front. My research has demonstrated that by the end of 2016 there had been 34 ISIS or ISIS-linked plots carried out by teens or pre-teens in seven different countries in the West.

Chairman Gallagher, distinguished Members of the committee, the risk that returning foreign fighters pose to the West is stark and will continue to be felt for many years to come. Countries impacted by this threat must continue to work together to mitigate this.

Thank you for inviting me today, and I look forward to your questions.

[The prepared statement of Mr. Simcox follows:]

PREPARED STATEMENT OF ROBIN SIMCOX

JULY 13, 2017

Chairman Gallagher and distinguished Members of the committee, thank you for the opportunity to testify here today.

My name is Robin Simcox; I am the Margaret Thatcher Fellow at The Heritage Foundation. My responsibilities consist of research on terrorist groups, particularly those targeting Europe, as well as research on intelligence and security policy. These are issues I have helped governments across Europe shape their response to for almost 10 years. I also regularly speak to relevant U.S. Government agencies on such matters.

The views I express in this testimony are my own and do not represent the official position of The Heritage Foundation.

My goal this afternoon is to highlight the ways in which fighters returning from Syria and Iraq pose a clear risk to the West. I will focus particularly on the European component of this phenomenon.

There are three aspects to the threat which I will discuss today: The short term, medium term, and long term.

THE SHORT TERM

At least 5,000 to 6,000 Europeans have fought alongside ISIS and other Islamist groups in Syria and Iraq.[1] Some have already been killed in the fighting, and as ISIS' "Caliphate" in Iraq and Syria comes under increasing pressure, yet more will be.

However, there is also an expectation that many foreign fighters will disperse, and inevitably, some of these individuals will return to their home countries. There could be approximately 1,000 returnees just from the United Kingdom, France, and Germany.

The risk posed by these returning fighters is clear. They will have fought in the Iraq/Syria conflicts and been trained by ISIS, al-Qaeda, or associated groups.

Indeed, the danger these fighters pose has already been demonstrated on the streets of Europe. Members of the cell that committed ISIS' attacks in Paris in November 2015—killing 130 and wounding 368—had traveled to Syria from Europe, fought and trained with ISIS, and then returned to Europe to carry out an attack. This cell also contained ISIS members who had entered Europe from Syria after making false asylum claims.

Those plugged into the same network then committed the attacks in Brussels in March 2016, which killed 32 and wounded approximately 300.

It is worth noting that American citizens were killed in both the Paris and Brussels attacks. Clearly, the threat to life of American lives is not consigned solely to the homeland.

THE MEDIUM TERM

Even if these returning fighters do not immediately plan to carry out terrorist attacks in the West, that does not mean they are not still detrimental to National security. These fighters will not be returning into a vacuum; they will be reconnecting with pre-existing Islamist networks. The United Kingdom, for example, has approximately 23,000 terror suspects on the intelligence radar.[2]

How these pre-existing radical networks will treat returning fighters from Syria will likely differ on a case-by-case basis. Yet we must remember that those who fought in previous foreign conflicts—such as Afghanistan in the 1980's and Bosnia in the 1990's—earned gravitas and credibility as heroic, returning members of the *mujahideen*. This helped propel a younger generation toward radicalism.

Take the example of a British citizen, Babar Ahmad. Ahmad, who pleaded guilty to terrorism offenses in the United States in 2013, fought in Bosnia in the 1990's and then returned to London. True, he did not commit a terrorist attack there. However, he was able to leverage his experience fighting in Bosnia to become one of the key radicalizers in the entire country upon return. He was successful in inspiring a younger generation of potential radicals to take up the fight.

This included men such as Saajid Badat, who was drawn into Ahmad's circle in South London and then dispatched to Afghanistan to train with al-Qaeda.[3] Badat was assigned by al-Qaeda to be part of the same suicide bombing mission as the "shoe bomber" Richard Reid. He pleaded guilty in a U.K. court concerning his role in this plot in 2005.

THE LONG TERM

The conflict in Syria has helped ensure that the war with Islamism will be a multi-generational one. Entire families from the West, including children, moved to Syria to live in the "Caliphate." Furthermore, there have been children born in

---

[1] "More than 6,000 European Jihadists in Syria, EU Official Says," *The Telegraph*, April 13, 2015, *http://www.telegraph.co.uk/news/worldnews/middleeast/syria/11531884/More-than-6000-European-jihadists-in-Syria-EU-official-says.html* (accessed June 21, 2017).

[2] Sean O'Neill, Fiona Hamilton, Fariha Karim, and Gabriella Swerling, "Huge Scale of Terror Threat Revealed: UK Home to 23,000 Jihadists," *The Times*, May 27, 2017, *https://www.thetimes.co.uk/article/huge-scale-of-terror-threat-revealed-uk-home-to-23-000-jihadists-3zvn58mhq* (accessed June 21, 2017).

[3] *United States* v. *Adis Medunjanin*, March 29, 2012, *https://www.documentcloud.org/documents/1048734-deposition-in-u-s-v-adis-medunjanin.html* (accessed July 6, 2017).

Syria to Western parents who may now be attempting to return to Europe. Many will have inevitably been indoctrinated with ISIS' ideology.

To use France as an example: There are almost 500 children currently in Syria with connections to France. Approximately 150 such children have been born there. There are approximately 80 Dutch children born in the "Caliphate";[4] and as many as 50 from the United Kingdom.[5]

How many of these children will end up returning to the West is at present unknowable. Yet knowing how to deal with the potential security threat from children of hardened ISIS fighters is clearly a major, long-term problem for Western governments.

Europol has warned that ISIS has demonstrated "that they train these minors to become the next generation of foreign terrorist fighters" and that this "may pose a future security threat to member states."[6] According to a report from the British counter-extremism think tank, Quilliam, "Boys learn a rigid Islamic State curriculum . . . Children churn out memorised verses of the Qur'an and attend 'Jihadist Training', which includes shooting, weaponry and martial arts."[7]

Furthermore, my previous research demonstrates that there is already a pre-existing threat to the West from teens and pre-teens. By the end of 2016, there had been 34 such plots carried out by this demographic in seven different countries.[8]

Chairman Gallagher, distinguished Members of the committee, the risk that returning foreign fighters pose to the West is stark and will continue to be felt for many years to come. Countries impacted by this threat must continue to work together to mitigate this. Even then, however, we can only reduce the risk, not eliminate it.

Thank you for inviting me today and I look forward to your questions.

Mr. GALLAGHER. Thank you, Mr. Simcox.

The Chair now recognizes Dr. Clarke for 5 minutes for an opening statement.

STATEMENT OF COLIN P. CLARKE, POLITICAL SCIENTIST, THE RAND CORPORATION

Mr. CLARKE. Thank you, Chairman Gallagher, Ranking Member Watson Coleman, and distinguished Members of the task force for inviting me to testify today.

My testimony will address three fundamental issues. First, what is the terrorist diaspora?

Second, what are the implications of this diaspora or more precisely what is the threat posed by returning foreign terrorist fighters?

Third, what can the United States do to mitigate the threat posed by foreign fighters fleeing the battlefield in Iraq and Syria?

The term terrorist diaspora as currently used more accurately describes foreign fighters who travel from more than 80 different countries to fight with militant groups in Iraq and Syria and who have moved on or soon will move on to other countries.

While some of these fighters might go on to provide support to Salafi-jihadist insurgencies, the part of the terrorist diaspora we are most concerned about are the foreign fighters who will move on

---

[4] Emily Feldman, "Can ISIS's Indoctrinated Kids Be Saved from a Future of Violent Jihad?" *Newsweek*, July 6, 2017, *http://www.newsweek.com/2017/07/14/isis-kids-indoctrination-saved-violent-jihad-632080.html* (accessed July 6, 2017).

[5] Noman Benotman and Nikita Malik, *The Children of Islamic State* (London: Quilliam, 2016).

[6] Lizzie Dearden, "ISIS Training Children of Foreign Fighters to Become 'Next Generation' of Terrorists," *The Independent*, July 29, 2016, *http://www.independent.co.uk/news/world/middle-east/isis-training-children-of-foreign-fighters-to-become-next-generation-of-terrorists-a7162911.html* (accessed July 6, 2017).

[7] Benotman and Malik, *The Children of Islamic State*.

[8] Robin Simcox, "The Islamic State's Western Teenage Plotters," *CTC Sentinel*, Vol. 10, No. 2 (February 2017), p. 21, *https://www.ctc.usma.edu/posts/the-islamic-states-western-teenage-plotters* (accessed June 21, 2017).

from Syria and Iraq to participate in other civil wars or organized terrorist cells that plot to attack the West.

So what is the threat posed by foreign terrorist fighters? I foresee multiple categories. The hardcore fighters will likely remain in Iraq and Syria and look to join whatever the next iteration of the group becomes. In all likelihood, ISIS remnants in Iraq and Syria will hide, rest, rearm, recuperate, going underground to reorganize before returning to wage the next phase of the insurgency.

A second group of fighters are the potential free agents or mercenaries who will travel abroad to take part in the next jihadist theater, whether it be in Yemen, Libya, the Caucuses, West Africa, or Afghanistan.

ISIS affiliates and local Sunni jihadists would likely welcome an influx of battle-hardened fighters. These fighters are the militant progeny of the original Mujahedeen, the transnational jihadists that once filled the ranks of al-Qaeda and fought in Afghanistan, Chechnya, and the Balkans.

A third group of foreign fighters, the returnees, has occupied much time and energy in policy and law enforcement circles. These fighters may attempt to return to their countries of origin, whether within the region to countries like Tunisia and Saudi Arabia or further afield to Europe, Asia, and North America.

This third group is not as homogeneous as it may seem. Just as foreign fighters who travel to Syria and Iraq left for different reasons and fought with different groups, those that return will do so for varying reasons as well.

The first subgroup of returnees might be labeled the disillusioned. These individuals went to Syria looking for Utopia, adventure, and a pure expression of religious identity, but they found something far different.

The second subgroup is the disengaged but not disillusioned. These militants, however, are still committed to jihadism. Although these militants might have grown disillusioned with ISIS as an organization, they still believe in the concept of jihad and remain committed to holy war against the West.

The final subgroup is called the operational returnees. These are the returning fighters who may attempt to resuscitate dormant networks or create new ones, recruit members, or conduct lone wolf-style attacks.

They could very well be prepositioned and seek to attempt an attack under the command and control of ISIS remnants in the Middle East. These individuals are the most dangerous and deadly.

The threat is far more serious for Europe and the Middle East than for the United States. The same factors that make Europe so vulnerable to the threat posed by foreign fighters, geography, the overall number of citizens who travel to Iraq and Syria, counterterrorism capabilities, poor continent-wide information sharing and intelligence and law enforcement coordination, and the relationship between Muslim communities and host nation governments are those same things that present favorably to the United States.

The United States must continue to allocate sufficient resources to prevent any foreign terrorist fighters from attempting to sneak into the country. This includes not only a stout defense of American borders, but also intelligence sharing with allies overseas, including European countries, Turkey, and other nations throughout the Middle East, Africa, and Asia.

While we must continue to prevent foreign terrorist fighters from attempting to return to the United States, we must also focus on the more likely threat posed by radicalization and home-grown violent extremism.

Countering violent extremism has proceeded in fits and starts in the West, including in the United States. We have too little data to understand which programs work well and which do not. Continued Federal support for on-going and future research will be critical to making progress in this area, as will oversight, monitoring, evaluation, and assessment to discern which programs work and why.

We are entering yet another period of uncertainty. With the dissolution of the geographic entity known as the ISIS caliphate, new threats and challenges will arise. Hearings such as this one and many others of its kind underscore just how seriously the United States takes these challenges.

The threat of terrorism can sometimes feel ubiquitous and how we communicate about terrorism and terrorist attacks affects how Americans assess the risk of terrorism. It is important to keep this overall perspective.

In short, I believe that the danger posed by ISIS to the U.S. homeland is real but manageable, but also sympathize with recent remarks offered by Lieutenant General Nagata that with respect to ISIS, we have to conclude that we do not fully appreciate the scale or strength of this phenomenon.

Thank you for the opportunity to testify today.

[The prepared statement of Dr. Clarke follows:]

PREPARED STATEMENT OF COLIN P. CLARKE [1][2]

JULY 13, 2017

Thank you Chairman Gallagher, Ranking Member Watson Coleman, and distinguished Members of the task force for inviting me to testify today. My testimony will address three fundamental issues. First, what is the terrorist diaspora? Second, what are the implications of this diaspora, or more precisely, what is the threat posed by returning foreign terrorist fighters? Third, what can the United States do to mitigate the threat posed by foreign fighters fleeing the battlefield in Iraq and Syria?

In September 2016, referring to the Islamic State in Iraq and Syria (ISIS), then-Federal Bureau of Investigation (FBI) Director James Comey acknowledged "the so-called caliphate will be crushed," although he subsequently warned that its fighters "will not all die on the battlefield in Syria and Iraq" and the result "will be a terrorist diaspora sometime in the next 2 to 5 years like we've never seen before."[3] The caliphate is indeed being crushed, but the second- and third-order effects of its deterioration could send shockwaves throughout the West, as surviving foreign fighters attempt to wreak havoc elsewhere.

---

[1] The opinions and conclusions expressed in this testimony are the author's alone and should not be interpreted as representing those of the RAND Corporation or any of the sponsors of its research.

[2] The RAND Corporation is a research organization that develops solutions to public policy challenges to help make communities throughout the world safer and more secure, healthier, and more prosperous. RAND is nonprofit, nonpartisan, and committed to the public interest.

[3] Josh Gerstein and Jennifer Scholtes, "Comey Warns of Post-ISIL Terrorist 'Diaspora,'" *Politico,* September 27, 2016.

ISIS is hemorrhaging territory, its financing continues to be degraded, and popular support for the group has diminished significantly.[4] As operations against ISIS in Mosul conclude and the offensive against the ISIS capital in Raqqa gains momentum, the terrorist group has begun shifting men and materiel to its stronghold in Deir Ezzor and Mayadeen, foreshadowing a potentially bloody conflict closer to the Iraqi and Jordanian borders.

For months, ISIS fighters have been reinfiltrating towns and villages throughout the Euphrates River Valley that were thought to have been cleared.[5] Furthermore, it is likely that hundreds of militants, including many foreign fighters, have already scattered elsewhere and are preparing to continue waging jihad in another theater.

WHAT IS THE TERRORIST DIASPORA?

The term diaspora, in its most fundamental sense, refers to a national, cultural, or religious group living in a foreign land. Historically, many diasporas have left their mark on overseas conflicts by providing both active and passive support—from Irish-Americans in the United States to Sri Lankan Tamils living in Canada.[6] But the term "terrorist diaspora," as currently used, more accurately describes foreign fighters who traveled from more than 80 different countries to fight with militant groups in Iraq and Syria and who have moved on or soon will move on to other countries. While some of these fighters might go on to provide passive support to Salafi-jihadist insurgencies,[7] the part of the "terrorist diaspora" we are most concerned about are the foreign fighters who will move on from Syria and Iraq to participate in other civil wars or organize terrorist cells.

An unprecedented number of fighters joined the battle in Iraq and Syria—many more than the mujahideen guerillas who fought in the Soviet-Afghan conflict during the 1980's. Jihadist expert Thomas Hegghammer estimated the number of foreign fighters in Afghanistan during the anti-Soviet conflict at 5,000 to 20,000,[8] while scholars such as Edwin Bakker and Mark Singleton have estimated that around 30,000 foreign fighters have fought in Iraq and Syria.[9] Thus, the wave of fighters who could emerge from the conflict is especially foreboding. Foreign fighters from the Afghan conflict went on to form the core of al-Qaeda and fight in the internecine conflicts in Bosnia and Herzegovina, Algeria, and Chechnya during the 1990's.[10] The fighters emerging from this conflict seek to leave a similar legacy.

Where do these foreign fighters come from? The Soufan Group estimates that approximately 6,000 are from the West; of these, roughly 150 are from the United States and 5,000 are from Western Europe. Nearly three-quarters of Western European fighters hail from just four countries: France (1,800), the United Kingdom (760), Germany (760), and Belgium (470).[11]

---

[4] Seth G. Jones, James Dobbins, Daniel Byman, Christopher S. Chivvis, Ben Connable, Jeffrey Martini, Eric Robinson, and Nathan Chandler, *Rolling Back the Islamic State,* Santa Monica, Calif.: RAND Corporation, RR–1912, 2017, See also David Francis, "Islamic State Revenues Down 80 Percent from 2015," *Foreign Policy,* June 29, 2017.

[5] Loveday Morris, "Away From Iraq's Front Lines, the Islamic State is Creeping Back In," *Washington Post,* February 22, 2017.

[6] Daniel Byman, Peter Chalk, Bruce Hoffman, William Rosenau, and David Brannan, *Trends in Outside Support for Insurgent Movements,* Santa Monica, Calif.: RAND Corporation, MR–1405–OTI, 2001.

[7] Salafi characterizes an adherent of an ideological strain in Sunni Islam that seeks to emulate, as purer, the thinking and practices of Muhammad and the earliest generations of Muslims. Jihadists believe that violent struggle against non-Muslims and Muslims they judge as apostate is an important religious duty (Benjamin W. Bahney, Howard J. Shatz, Carroll Ganier, Renny McPherson, Barbara Sude, with Sara Beth Elson, and Ghassan Schbley, *An Economic Analysis of the Financial Records of al-Qa'ida in Iraq,* Santa Monica, Calif.: RAND Corporation, MG–1026–OSD, 2010.

[8] Thomas Hegghammer, "The Rise of Muslim Foreign Fighters," International Security, Vol. 35, No. 3, Winter 2010/2011, pp. 53–94.

[9] Edwin Bakker and Mark Singleton, "Foreign Fighters in the Syria and Iraq Conflict: Statistics and Characteristics of a Rapidly Growing Phenomenon," in Andrea de Guttry, Francesca Capone, and Christophe Paulussen, eds., *Foreign Fighters Under International Law and Beyond,* The Hague: TMC Asser Press, 2016. Importantly, this number likely does not include the foreign fighters in Syria fighting against the Islamic State and al-Qaeda-linked groups like Jabhat al-Nusra (since rebranded Jabhat Fateh al-Sham). Indeed, significant numbers of Afghan and Pakistani Shia are also fighting alongside Hezbollah and other pro-Assad elements and could very well be a problem for the United States in future conflicts, especially as tensions continue to grow with Iran.

[10] R. Kim Cragin, "Early History of Al-Qa'ida," *The Historical Journal,* Vol. 51, No. 4, 2008, pp. 1047–1067.

[11] The Soufan Group, "Foreign Fighters: An Updated Assessment of the Flow of Foreign Fighters Into Syria and Iraq," December 8, 2015.

The foreign fighter phenomenon is likely to worsen in the future as the caliphate continues to deteriorate. This phenomenon is not new. Over the past 200 years, foreign fighters have appeared in more than a quarter of all civil wars.[12] However, this new generation of jihadists has improved communication, easier transportation, and diversified sources of information and money, making even small cadres of experienced fighters a dangerous force. These fighters can now engage in foreign civil wars and insurgencies—and export their expertise back to their home countries or to places they have newly immigrated. In addition, encrypted communications and the ubiquity of social media mean that even after the caliphate disappears, the ideology of Salafi-jihadism will persist on-line as a virtual caliphate, offering aspiring jihadists hope that the next major battle is all but inevitable and continuing to exhort its followers to conduct violence wherever they are.

WHAT IS THE THREAT POSED BY FOREIGN TERRORIST FIGHTERS?

Accordingly, what might ISIS' remaining foreign fighters choose to do next? When a conflict winds down, either through force or by negotiated settlement, where do transnational terrorists go? As I have outlined in *Foreign Policy* and *The Atlantic,* I see several possibilities.[13]

The "hardcore fighters" will likely remain in Iraq and Syria and look to join whatever the next iteration of the devolving group may be. In all likelihood, ISIS remnants in Iraq and Syria will hide, rest, rearm, and recuperate, going underground to reorganize before returning to wage the next phase of the insurgency.[14] In the interim, ISIS could transform into a clandestine terrorist organization, retaining the ability to conduct sporadic raids, ambushes, and possibly spectacular suicide attacks, both in the region and abroad.[15]

During this time, militants may switch allegiances among the hodgepodge of groups on the ground, including ISIS, Hayat Tahrir al-Sham,[16] and Ahrar al-Sham (which is already a loose coalition of Islamist and Salafist units), and will actively seek out ungoverned areas still outside of the writ of either Syrian or Iraqi government forces and their allies. As terrorism expert Bruce Hoffman has suggested, if the fortunes of ISIS continue to decline, some jihadists may see rapprochement with al-Qaeda as the only option to continue the struggle.[17] Another factor leading to a marriage of convenience between former comrades could be the death of ISIS leader Abu Bakr al-Baghdadi, leading to a new phase in the global jihad.[18]

A second group of fighters are the potential "free-agents or mercenaries," who will travel abroad to take part in the next jihadist theater, whether it be in Yemen, Libya, the Caucasus, West Africa, or Afghanistan. ISIS affiliates and local Sunni jihadists would likely welcome an influx of battle-hardened fighters. These fighters are the militant progeny of the original mujahideen, the transnational jihadists that once filled the ranks of al-Qaeda and fought in Afghanistan, Chechnya, and the Balkans. Some fighters who are prevented from returning to their home countries can be expected to form a cohort of state-less jihadists who deliberately seek out weakly-governed conflict zones in unstable regions.[19] World-wide attention has made such travel more difficult than for prior generations of extremists, but some will no doubt escape detection.

---

[12] David Malet, *Foreign Fighters: Transnational Identity in Civil Conflicts,* New York: Oxford University Press, 2013.

[13] Brian Michael Jenkins and Colin P. Clarke, "In the Event of the Islamic State's Untimely Demise," Foreign Policy, May 11, 2016; see also Colin P. Clarke and Amarnath Amarasingam, "Where Do ISIS Fighters Go When the Caliphate Falls?" *The Atlantic,* March 6, 2017.

[14] Colin P. Clarke and Craig Whiteside, "Charting the Future of the Modern Caliphate," *War on the Rocks,* May 3, 2017.

[15] Daniel Milton and Muhammad al-'Ubaydi, *The Fight Goes On: The Islamic State's Continuing Military Efforts in Liberated Cities,* Combating Terrorism Center (CTC) at West Point, June 2017. It is also worth noting that, while ISIS will still pose a threat as a clandestine terrorist organization, the trajectory is moving in the right direction, as the organization is sequentially downgraded from a caliphate to an insurgency to a terrorist group.

[16] Hayat Tahrir al-Sham is the rebranded Jabhat Fateh al-Sham, which itself was the rebranded al-Qaeda affiliate Jabhat al-Nusra. Hayat Tahrir al-Sham has disavowed a formal connection with al-Qaeda, but the true relationship between the groups is a matter of skepticism and debate.

[17] Bruce Hoffman, "Al-Qaeda: Quietly and Patiently Rebuilding," *The Cipher Brief,* December 30, 2016.

[18] Colin P. Clarke, "Is ISIS Leader Baghdadi Still Alive?" *Foreign Affairs,* June 22, 2017; see also, Colin P. Clarke, "Can the Islamic State Survive if Baghdadi is Dead?" *Foreign Policy,* June 30, 2017.

[19] David Malet, "Foreign Fighter Mobilization and Persistence in a Global Context," *Terrorism and Political Violence,* Vol. 27, No. 3, 2015, pp.454–473.

When terrorism scholar Amarnath Amarasingam interviewed a Western ISIS fighter in late 2016, he emphasized the global reach of ISIS, saying the caliphate "has reached Afghanistan, Libya, West Africa, Algeria, Yemen, and many, many of its soldiers are in the lands of the [unbelievers]" (the West).[20] As ISIS loses territory in Iraq and Syria, some fighters may indeed try to reach these other theaters of jihad to protect, sustain, and expand the boundaries of the so-called caliphate. In other words, they see other potential options.

A third group of foreign fighters—the "returnees"—has occupied much time and energy in policy and law enforcement circles.[21] These fighters may attempt to return to their countries of origin, whether in the region to Tunisia and Saudi Arabia, or further afield to Europe, Asia, and North America. States with more robust national screening mechanisms, law enforcement, and intelligence structures stand a better chance of stopping the fighters at their border, blunting the impact of these returnees. But not all Western security services are created equal, and further complicating the issue is the inability to even agree on the definition of who constitutes a foreign fighter in the first place.[22]

This third group is not as homogenous as it may seem. Just as foreign fighters who traveled to Syria and Iraq left for different reasons and fought with different groups, those that return will do so for varying reasons as well.

The first subgroup of returnees might be labeled the "disillusioned." These individuals went to Syria looking for utopia, adventure, and a pure expression of religious identity,[23] but they found something far different. Local Syrians did not respect them. They struggled with food, financing, and the tribulations of war. Upon returning to the West, these individuals could mentor other radicalized youth. These fighters may require psychological treatment in addition to prison time.

The second subgroup is the "disengaged but not disillusioned." Just as there are many reasons why militants go to fight, there are many reasons why they leave a conflict—marriage, battle fatigue, desire to be with family.[24] These militants, however, are still committed to jihadism. Accordingly, individuals might grow disillusioned with ISIS as an organization, but not with jihad as a whole.

The final subgroup is called the "operational" returnees. These are returning fighters who attempt to resuscitate dormant or create new networks, recruit members, or conduct home-grown-style attacks. They are likely to be pre-positioned and likely to attempt an attack under the command and control of ISIS remnants in the Middle East.[25] These individuals are the most dangerous and deadly.[26] The November 2015 Paris attacks are perhaps the clearest example; they were conducted by foreign fighters, who were trained in Syria and dispatched to France.[27] Operational returnees are of even more concern if one believes that hundreds of operatives have already been deployed to Europe, with hundreds more hiding out on Europe's doorstep in Turkey.[28]

The West must develop a range of strategies to handle the threat posed by these different groups. The "hardcore fighters" who remain in Iraq and Syria will need to be killed or captured by Iraqi Security Forces and the anti-ISIS coalition. The first priority should be detection, which goes hand-in-hand with increased informa-

---

[20] Lorne L. Dawson and Amarnath Amarasingam, "Talking to Foreign Fighters: Insights Into the Motivation for Hijrah to Syria and Iraq," *Studies in Conflict & Terrorism,* Vol. 40, No. 3, 2017, pp. 191–210.

[21] R. Kim Cragin has argued that, contrary to popular belief, most foreign fighters do not die on battlefields or travel from conflict to conflict, but return home. See R. Kim Cragin, "The Challenge of Foreign Fighter Returnees," *Journal of Contemporary Criminal Justice,* 2017.

[22] Alastair Reed and Johanna Pohl, "Disentangling the EU Foreign Fighter Threat: The Case for a Comprehensive Approach," *RUSI,* February 10, 2017.

[23] Simon Cottee, "Pilgrims to the Islamic State," *The Atlantic,* July 24, 2015.

[24] Jessica Stern and J.M. Berger, "ISIS and the Foreign Fighter Phenomenon," *The Atlantic,* March 8, 2015.

[25] See Rukmini Callimachi, "Not 'Lone Wolves' After All: How ISIS Guides World's Terror Plots from Afar," *New York Times,* February 4, 2017; see also Daveed Gartenstein-Ross and Madeline Blackman, "ISIL's Virtual Planners: A Critical Terrorist Innovation," *War on the Rocks,* January 4, 2017; and Alexander Meleagrou-Hitchens and Seamus Hughes, "The Threat to the United States From the Islamic State's Virtual Entrepreneurs," *CTC Sentinel,* Vol. 10, No. 3, March 2017, pp. 1–8.

[26] Thomas Hegghammer, "Should I Stay Or Should I Go? Explaining Variation in Western Jihadists' Choice between Domestic and Foreign Fighting," *American Political Science Review,* Vol. 107, No. 1, February 2013, pp. 1–15.

[27] R. Kim Cragin, "The November 2015 Paris Attacks: The Impact of Foreign Fighter Returnees," *Orbis,* Vol. 61, No. 2, 2017, pp. 212–226.

[28] Rukmini Callimachi, "How a Secretive Branch of ISIS Built a Global Network of Killers," *New York Times,* August 3, 2016; see also Bruce Hoffman, "The Global Terror Threat and Counterterrorism Challenges Facing the Next Administration," *CTC Sentinel,* Vol. 9, No. 11, November/December 2016.

tion sharing and training partner nations to screen and investigate capacity potential terrorists. This suggests an even greater role for multilateral cooperation.

Another major hurdle will be marshaling the resources necessary to monitor, track, and surveil dozens of battle-hardened jihadists attempting to blend back into Western society. Combating the threat posed by the "free agents" or roving band of militants calls for continued efforts by the West to build the partner capacity of host-nation forces in weak and fragile States.

WHAT IS THE THREAT TO THE HOMELAND AND WHAT SHOULD THE UNITED STATES DO TO MITIGATE THE THREAT?

It is critical to have a judicious discussion about the threat posed to the U.S. homeland while avoiding arguments that present the issue as binary. In other words, defining the threat as either completely overwhelming or relatively nonexistent is myopic at best and counterproductive at worst. The threat to the West posed by returning foreign fighters is anything but monolithic.

It is prudent to discuss the longer-term consequences to the homeland of the unraveling so-called caliphate in Iraq and Syria. In the long term, military gains against ISIS are a necessary step in ultimately defeating it. But in the shorter term, its dissolution will create uncertainty, rising threats, opportunities for extremists, and new challenges for our military, intelligence, and law enforcement communities. I am comforted in knowing that much effort has been focused on this threat since the summer of 2014—testimonies by the FBI, the Central Intelligence Agency, the Director of National Intelligence, and others have reinforced that the United States has taken the threat seriously and been a leader in international cooperation to combat these foreign fighters. And despite the high casualties inflicted on fighters who went to Iraq and Syria, their sheer numbers means that the threat will be with us for years to come.

The threat is far more serious for Europe and the Middle East than for the United States. The same factors that make Europe so vulnerable to the threat posed by foreign fighters—geography; the number of citizens who traveled to Iraq or Syria; counterterrorism capabilities, including screening, watchlisting, and whole-of-government programs; poor continent-wide information sharing and intelligence and law-enforcement coordination; and the relationship between Muslim communities and host-nation governments—present favorably for the United States. As director of the National Counterterrorism Center (NCTC), Nicholas Rasmussen acknowledged in Congressional testimony that compared to European counterparts, U.S. ports of entry are under far less strain from migration and U.S. law enforcement agencies are not nearly as overtaxed by the sheer numbers of terrorist plots and potential suspects.[29]

Since the attacks of September 11, 2001, 95 Americans have died in jihadist-related attacks in the homeland, with 63 of those deaths coming from just two attacks—San Bernardino and Orlando. According to a recent report on radicalization and jihadist attacks in the West, of the 17 successful attacks linked to jihadist terrorists in the United States between June 2014 and June 2017, none were perpetrated by foreign fighters.[30] But Americans have gone to Syria and returned to the United States. A U.S. citizen from Florida, Moner Mohammad Abu-Salha, traveled to Syria to fight with al-Qaeda's affiliate organization and returned to the United States without U.S. officials realizing that he had trained with a terrorist group, proving that government and intelligence authorities are not omniscient.

Terrorists traveling to the United States from abroad to conduct attacks are still rare events. While 9/11 was undoubtedly a high-impact event, without question, it remains an anomaly. Moreover, since then, the United States has gone to great lengths to defend the homeland. The United States has worked with the screening community to develop a comprehensive, end-to-end vetting system that is part of a robust system of measures, including face-to-face interviews and biometric assessments, intended to serve as a line of defense against foreign fighters seeking to infiltrate the country.[31]

---

[29] Nicholas J. Rasmussen, "Fifteen Years After 9/11: Threats to the Homeland," Statement for the Record: Hearing Before the Senate Homeland Security Governmental Affairs Committee, September 27, 2016.

[30] Lorenzo Vidino, Francesco Marone, and Eva Entenmann, *Fear Thy Neighbor: Radicalization and Jihadist Attacks in the West,* Institute for International Political Studies, June 2017.

[31] For more on specific programs and databases, including the Terrorist Identities Datamart Environment, the Transportation Security Administration's Automated Targeting System, and the Electronic System for Travel Authorization, see Brian Michael Jenkins, "There Will Be Battles in the Heart of Your Abode: The Threat Posed by Foreign Fighters Returning from Syria

Continued

Even with these measures, the threat has atomized; in the United States, violence perpetrated by home-grown violent extremists (HVEs) remains perhaps our foremost concern. The FBI has investigations on approximately 1,000 potential HVEs across all 50 States. As ISIS continues to lose territory, it will likely seek to emphasize high-profile attacks to remain relevant and demonstrate virility in the face of severe adversity. This could result in an uptick in lone-wolf attacks in the West, including in the United States. Put simply, what happens in Raqqa matters in Rochester.

Comparing the current threat level in the United States to the immediate aftermath of 9/11, Rasmussen observed,

"The threat landscape is less predictable and, while the scale of capabilities currently demonstrated by most of the violent extremist actors does not rise to the level that core al-Qaeda had on 9/11, it is fair to say that we face more threats originating in more places and involving more individuals than we have at any time in the past 15 years."[32]

Accordingly, the United States must continue to allocate sufficient resources to preventing foreign terrorist fighters from attempting to sneak into the country. This includes not only a stout defense of American borders, but also intelligence sharing with allies overseas, including European countries, Turkey, and other nations throughout the Middle East, Africa, and Asia.

And while we must continue to prevent foreign terrorist fighters from attempting to return to the United States, we must also focus on the more likely threat posed by radicalization and home-grown violent extremism. Countering violent extremism has proceeded in fits and starts in the West, including in the United States. We have too little data to understand which programs work well and which do not—continued Federal support for on-going and future research will be critical to making progress in this area, as will oversight, monitoring, evaluation, and assessment to discern which programs work and why.[33]

We still understand very little about the radicalization process, what role the internet and social media play in this process, and what policy should be when it comes to monitoring terrorist use of social media (e.g., is it more prudent to shut communication channels down or leave them up to monitor and map terrorist networks?) Congress might consider funding more fusion cells and allocating resources for law enforcement training to deal with the threat from returning foreign fighters. This could extend to funding for the recruitment of linguists and cultural experts working in tandem with Customs and Border Patrol and Citizenship and Immigration Services.

CONCLUSION

We are entering yet another period of uncertainty. With the dissolution of the geographic entity known as the ISIS caliphate, new threats and challenges will arise. Hearings such as this and many others of its kind underscore how seriously the United States takes these challenges. The threat of terrorism can sometimes feel ubiquitous, especially as "the post-9/11 media has profoundly changed how Americans assess the risk of terrorism."[34] It is important to keep a sober perspective.

In their 2015 study, "Assessing the Islamic State's Commitment to Attacking the West," Hegghammer and Petter Nesser conclude that "the Islamic State does not currently pose the same type of terrorist threat to the West as al-Qaeda did in the 2000's."[35] I would extrapolate on this to argue that this statement may be true for the United States, but perhaps no longer true for Europe. But even within the United States, there are risks that may not stem from the terrorist diaspora.

And while we focus on these new challenges posed by the unraveling of ISIS, let us not forget that our principal terrorist adversary over the past 20 years—al-Qaeda (or at least some form of it), is still with us, as evidenced by al-Qaeda in the Arabian Peninsula's increasing obsession with attacking commercial aviation; this group will remain a direct threat to the United States.

---

and Iraq," testimony presented before the Senate Homeland Security and Governmental Affairs Committee on March 12, 2015.

[32] Rasmussen, 2016.

[33] An especially promising study is Todd Helmus, Miriam Matthews, Rajeev Ramchand, Sina Beaghley, David Stebbins, Amanda Kadlec, Michael A. Brown, Aaron Kofner, and Joie D. Acosta, *RAND Program Evaluation Toolkit for Countering Violent Extremism,* Santa Monica, Calif.: RAND Corporation, TL–243–DHS, 201.

[34] Daniel Byman and Will McCants, "Fight of Flight: How to Avoid a Forever War Against Jihadists," *Washington Quarterly,* No. 40, No. 2, 2017, pp.67–77.

[35] Thomas Hegghammer and Peter Nesser, "Assessing the Islamic State's Commitment to Attacking the West," *Perspectives on Terrorism,* Vol. 9, No. 4, 2015.

With each brutal battle in Iraq and Syria, the potential pool of foreign fighters is shrinking. ISIS fighters are dying in shocking numbers—nearly 60,000 have died since June 2014.[36] The 300 that until recently were hunkered down in Mosul showed no proclivity to surrender or escape; they launched counteroffensives against Iraqi forces, including waves of suicide attackers. Those that survive these major battles will keep defending the caliphate until the bitter end, either in Mayadeen or in whatever disparate outposts of the Sunni Arab hinterlands remain available.

In short, I agree with the assessment of Georgetown University professor Daniel Byman, who, in testimony last month to the U.S. Senate Committee on Foreign Relations, concluded the danger posed by ISIS to the U.S. homeland is "real but manageable."[37] With 150 American foreign fighters, scores of whom are presumably dead, it may be possible to assign regular surveillance to each of these individuals in case they do attempt to return home.

Yet even as the United States faces less of a threat than our European allies, we cannot become complacent and must ensure continued vigilance. Toward this end, I heed recent remarks offered by Lt. Gen. Michael K. Nagata, one of the Army's top special operations forces officers, that with respect to ISIS, "we have to conclude that we do not fully appreciate the scale or strength of this phenomenon."[38]

Mr. GALLAGHER. Thank you, Dr. Clarke.

In the interest of time, Member questioning will be limited to 3 minutes each with multiple rounds if possible. Without objection, so ordered.

I now recognize myself for 3 minutes for questioning. The primary purpose of this task force is denying terrorist entry into the United States, obviously, but what emerges from all of your testimony is, in my opinion, the urgent threat that our European allies—I think Mr. Simcox, you threw out the figure of 23,000 suspects in the United Kingdom.

Maybe each of you briefly, could you address what steps our European allies have taken in terms of identifying and fixing gaps in screening, border security, information sharing, prosecution, and where they might need to go?

Mr. JOSCELYN. I will just add one quick response to that. One of the things in the Europol report that I pointed to, which I flagged for you in my written testimony, is that they are putting more investigators in the refugee hotspots pouring in through Italy and the Mediterranean and Greece and that sort of thing to try and figure out basically which ones are actually foreign fighters who were trying to use the refugee flows as a mask for their own operations, sort of as the Paris in November 2015 attackers did.

I think what Robin pointed to and some of the other statistics I point to in my report that the main problem here is that European counterterrorism forces are basically—authorities are overwhelmed. They are trying to basically look at a vast threat pool, and they are trying to determine which ones are going to pop off at any given time.

The link I wanted to highlight there was I think it is easier for European citizens or residents to get into this country if they wanted to come here and do an attack than somebody who wanted to come directly from Iraq and Syria or possibly one of these other hotspots.

Mr. SIMCOX. So the Europeans have got better at sharing intelligence when it comes to the foreign terrorist fighter threat, but

---

[36] Ben Hubbard and Eric Schmitt, "ISIS, Despite Heavy Losses, Still Inspires Global Attacks," *New York Times,* July 8, 2017.

[37] Daniel Byman, "Beyond Iraq and Syria: ISIS' Ability to Conduct Attacks Abroad," testimony for the U.S. Senate Committee on Foreign Relations, June 8, 2017.

[38] Hubbard and Schmitt, 2017.

where there hasn't been an awful lot of progress and where there is inconsistency is the non-foreign fighters, the radicals that are already in that country.

Say, are the Dutch sharing information with the United Kingdom? Are the United Kingdom sharing the information with France? Often they can't because of the nature of how that intelligence has been gathered. So there is a real problem, not from the screening refugees problem, is still a major issue because of the scale of the numbers that are still coming in. I think there is a lot more that needs to be done on that.

But I would just say in my conversations with European officials they know that their capacity on this isn't good enough. They want help on it, and it is a real area of potential agreement and cooperation between the United States and the European partners who want to get better.

Mr. CLARKE. My conversations I know the Europeans are working hard to build capacity in those areas, including training. But one area in particular, and I tend to focus a lot on the finance end of attacks, is synching law enforcement at the local level with the National-level entities.

A lot of these jihadis have criminal backgrounds. Sometimes these are guys that are petty thieves and criminals and they are more well-known to the local beat cops than they are at the higher level. So connecting those two from the grassroots up to the top is critical to figuring out exactly who these people are and how they may attempt to fund their attacks.

We know how they funded their travel to Iraq and Syria. We are now concerned about how they might fund their travel from Iraq and Syria back home to Belgium, the United Kingdom, France, Germany, et cetera.

Mr. GALLAGHER. Great, thank you.

To my colleagues 3 minutes goes quickly, so use it wisely.

The Chair now—but I do hope we are able to touch on both of your testimonies touch on the cubs of the caliphate program and the role of children, as well as domestic radicalization, which is a real thorny one.

But the Chair now recognizes the Ranking Member of the task force Mrs. Watson Coleman——

Mrs. WATSON COLEMAN. Thank you very much.

Mr. GALLAGHER [continuing]. For 3 minutes.

Mrs. WATSON COLEMAN. Thank you for your testimony. I think I want to follow up with what the Chairman was talking about. You talked about the impact on our European partners.

What is it that we can do that European partners would allow us to do that would help them in what really becomes a crisis for them and that would therefore accrue a benefit to us by ensuring that what is happening there is documenting, is accountable, and makes us safer?

I would like to hear from each of you on that. I guess that will be my 3 minutes.

Mr. JOSCELYN. OK. Real quick, I will just say the United States is the best in the world at tracking the external attack network for ISIS, which are the plotters who are actually trying to send people abroad to commit attacks. It is some of that intelligence I would imagine is probably highly classified and difficult to share.

But what is imperative there is to try and identify the external attack planners and figure out any of the Europeans or Western citizens or people in their orbit who may be tied to their networks who then could be activated abroad or could be sent abroad for an attack. That is sort-of a key link, I think, in terms of the severity of terrorist plots.

Mr. SIMCOX. I would suggest there are a couple of things. For example, one of the problems that European countries are having is when people, for example, from Tunisia have come into their countries illegally, they are having tremendous problems being able to send them back if they are a National security threat.

So any pressure the pressure the United States can put on some of those countries to be able to get them to accept security threats from Europe would be a great help.

Sharing intelligence where possible, although I know of course it isn't always possible, it is very useful. Encouraging European governments to spend money on this, encouraging them to treat it with the seriousness it deserves, especially some of the smaller European countries.

I think overall just taking a more aggressive and realistic approach to the issue. It seems hard to believe that Europe didn't before 2016, but I think that is the reality in some of those countries.

Mr. CLARKE. I think as Tom mentioned, I would echo the United States is the best in the world at screening, watchlisting, and connecting what we are doing offensively in the region in Iraq and Syria with what we are trying to do defensively in terms of securing borders at home.

One area I think that the Europeans could probably use some advice is in triangulating intelligence, right? So all the different "INTS" that we know and talk about, SIGINT, HUMINT, and everything else, because it has got to be really a multi-INT picture instead of looking at these in individual siloes.

Mrs. WATSON COLEMAN. Do you believe that the current climate with sort-of our leadership at the very top and the way we have been dealing with our so-called allies on the international stage has any impact at all on whether or not they would be amenable to our assistance?

Mr. JOSCELYN. Well, there is a lot to answer there, ma'am, and I don't have enough time, but I will just say one thing. The leaks that we saw coming out about the investigations in the United Kingdom around the Manchester arena bombing, which is not directly tied to politics but is tied to intel sharing, did cause problems. That sort of thing needs to be tamped down permanently.

Mr. GALLAGHER. Thank you.

The Chair now recognizes the gentleman from Louisiana, Captain Higgins.

Mr. HIGGINS. Thank you, Mr. Chairman. Gentlemen from the panel, thank you for appearing.

I believe that terrorists overseas that are identified as active, radicalized, Islamic jihadists should be tracked and killed. I believe we should identify and very closely monitor suspected radicalized Islamic terrorists. If it can be determined that they are involved in conspiracy to commit actual acts of terror, then they should be arrested, prosecuted, and if convicted, incarcerated.

I further believe that we need to stop or greatly interfere with the recruitment and radicalization efforts that are taking place as we defeat our enemy and it disperses, which is the essence of this particular hearing. They are recruiting new people. This is increasingly happening in the digital realm.

So this leads me to my question for you, Mr. Joscelyn. Do you believe that the United States and our allies are sufficiently monitoring and defending our homelands, our respective homelands, as allies in regarding the digital realm, including monitoring social media, emails, et cetera, to stop radicalization efforts?

That the time is coming fast when a man would have to travel to a foreign land to receive training in jihadist training. It could be done on-line. Are we doing what we need to do to stop that?

Mr. JOSCELYN. I don't have enough time to give you a full answer. Maybe I will do something in writing, but there is a mixed bag is the answer basically.

The FBI and others inside the United States do some amazing work in thwarting plots. If you go through their filings and legal filings in terms of detecting email traffic and that sort of thing in finding people who are radicalized and who are in communication with ISIS operatives overseas. There is some amazing work being done there.

In terms of counter-messaging though, however, in the digital websites and social media and that and shutting that down, however, I would say no. The efforts don't come close to being adequate to what they should be.

Mr. HIGGINS. Thank you.

Mr. JOSCELYN. If I can find the ISIS propaganda sites, if Calipha News 381 is suspended at 12:01, I know Calipha News 382 is up at 12:02. Doesn't take me much to find it, you know? So they know that, too. So there are a lot of problems in that regard.

Mr. HIGGINS. Would you be able to give this committee a more thorough answer in writing, sir, whereby we may examine your suggestions and consider them?

Mr. JOSCELYN. I would be happy to.

Mr. HIGGINS. Thank you very much.

Mr. Chairman, I yield back.

Mr. GALLAGHER. The Chair now recognizes the gentlelady from California, Ms. Barragán for 3 minutes.

Ms. BARRAGÁN. Thank you.

Mr. Clarke, the administration earlier this year instituted a travel ban that impacted mostly majority-Muslim countries. What is your opinion? Do you happen to think that a ban like this only exacerbates the threat of foreign fighters coming back? If so, why?

Mr. CLARKE. I think it is still too early to tell what the impact of a potential ban is. In general I think it is a good idea to constantly reassess who we let into this country, so I do agree with taking a hard look and scrutinizing who travels to this country.

But at the same time, there is a threat from countries like Pakistan, Afghanistan, and elsewhere that weren't included on the travel ban. So I think right now—again, there is also a lag effect in terms of a lot of this, how it is portrayed from a propaganda perspective. But again, a lot of things that the United States does is included in propaganda.

So again, at the end of the day I think I would probably leave it as an incomplete. I think this is a period right now where we are in a pause, where we have an opportunity to look further and to see how effective this actually could be.

Ms. BARRAGÁN. OK.

My next question for anybody is if foreign fighters are returned to the United States by what mode or means do you think they will return? What is the most likely? Would it be, you know, planes, airports, the port through board, on foot through that south border wall? I mean, if you are going to have ISIS fighters come to this country by what mode do you think it would be most likely to come back?

Mr. JOSCELYN. I mean, I think it probably they would try—the normal means that we all use to try to get back in the country I think is probably the way they go, flights, that sort of thing. I don't see any data that is publicly available that says they are preferring one means over another, you know, if that is what you are asking.

So there is no policy justification for trying to block one means versus another one, if that is what you are asking, as far as I can tell.

Ms. BARRAGÁN. Does anybody else want to chime in?

Mr. CLARKE. In terms of how jihadists or foreign terrorist fighters may attempt to infiltrate, yes, I think most likely they are going to try to fly here, but again, it is often presented as a binary debate.

I hear all the time that it is framed in terms of there are terrorists pouring over the border or no, they would never come over the Southern Border. I don't see evidence that there are terrorists pouring over the border, but at the same time it seems logical that that would be one way to sneak into the country.

So my follow-up to that is always if someone were to infiltrate the country through the Mexican border, is there an existing infrastructure in place that would facilitate some kind of attack? I am far more doubtful about that.

So if they were to go through the trouble of getting here, then what? I often don't hear a good response to that.

Mr. GALLAGHER. Thank you.

The Chair now recognizes the gentleman from Florida, Mr. Rutherford for 3 minutes.

Mr. RUTHERFORD. Thank you, Mr. Chairman.

Mr. Clarke, in your written testimony you had talked about really three types of fighters, the hardcore, the free agents, the mercenary types, and then also the returnees, as you call them.

I am particularly concerned about the returnees who could come back to the United States, but could you talk about the breakdown of what you suspect that might look like? How many will actually remain hardcore in the region? How many will, do you think return?

Mr. CLARKE. Yes. So it is difficult to quantify that, right, to say I think 30 percent are going to stay, you know, 20 percent—any number I gave you would be made up. I think by and large those that are committed to the fight, as we have seen in Mosul, have dug in and are fighting to the death.

A lot of foreign fighters, including a lot of Chechens have stayed, and they are meeting their death in Mosul. I think, again, due to geography it would be difficult for those that wanted to get back to the United States to do so.

So I think the second-most likely category is probably the free agents and mercenaries who go on and fight another fight, whether that is in Libya, whether that is in other parts of North Africa or elsewhere.

So I think the returnees are probably the smallest percentage. But as research by Thomas Hegghammer and others have shown, those that do make the trip back that are trained are the most lethal. So while it is a small chance or a small percentage, we still have to obviously guard against that.

Mr. RUTHERFORD. Right. I particularly want to highlight that you said they are the most lethal. Which makes it imperative that we do all that we can to battlefield identify those individuals in all three groups because, as you said, we don't really know who will be in which group.

But Mr. Simcox, can you talk a little bit about how we are doing as far as battlefield identification of individuals and getting them into the terrorist system so that CBP and others know who these folks are when they start to travel?

Mr. SIMCOX. Well, certainly from a European perspective, they are very confident that they know who most of the people are who have traveled. They are never going to get complete coverage, but they are quite confident.

I think one of the things to look for when you are trying to assess and as Dr. Clarke said, it is very hard to know exactly who is going to pose the most lethal threat upon return and quantify it, but it is worth looking, I think, at when people traveled. Anyone traveling to Syria after 2014 at the latest knew what he was or she was going there to get involved in. They knew what ISIS represented.

You could make an argument for maybe some of the 2011 travelers had different motivation, so I think it is borderline. But you could make an argument. So I do think it is worth looking at the dates of departure when trying to assess this.

Mr. RUTHERFORD. Thank you, Mr. Chairman. I yield back.

Mr. GALLAGHER. Thank you.

The Chair now recognizes the gentlelady from Texas, Ms. Jackson Lee for 3 minutes.

Ms. JACKSON LEE. Let me thank the Chairman for yielding and thank the Ranking Member as well.

The witnesses, I was in a similar hearing this morning so I am just going to follow the same tracking of questions. I like the opening statement that I am reading that indicates "The fall of Mosul and likely of Raqqa won't be the end of the Islamic State." I said this morning that our responsibilities are clearly the securing of the homeland.

So I would be interested in your assessment of intelligence resources and how you think we should emphasize intelligence resources in terms of the preventative blocking or intelligence about how many recruits may return or the idea of surveilling and determining—obviously we are a freedom of speech and thought Nation—those who may be radicalized right here in the United States off of social media.

Mr. Joscelyn.

Mr. JOSCELYN. Just real quick, that opening line was from my testimony, and the thought that leads off from——

Ms. JACKSON LEE. I was wondering if you would recognize it.

Mr. JOSCELYN. I did.

Main reason is because we are talking about the terrorist diaspora today. I think Robin in his testimony emphasized parts of this as well. I don't think it is going to be a shotgun blast of a diaspora out of the lands of the caliphate where you have to deal with it sort of all at once.

I think this is going to be an on-going problem for intelligence and homeland security officials, you know, in the near future. You have multilayers to the problem. Yes, you have the perspective of a guy or a gal who basically comes back directly to commit an attack that day or that week or that month.

That is probably a low percentage of overall what you are going to be dealing with in the long run. The long run you have to worry about those sort of second-tier threats, the people who are going to come back and do, as Robin talked about, indoctrinating or recruiting a cell.

There is an example I wrote up recently of somebody who came from al-Qaeda in Syria back to Columbus, Ohio or somewhere in Ohio and basically he was setting up a cell to commit an attack. He wasn't even going to do it himself.

That sort of thing is, I think, in the long run what is going to basically take up probably more resources than is probably appreciated right now.

Ms. JACKSON LEE. Thank you.

Mr. Simcox.

Mr. SIMCOX. Well, I think you obviously need to take a board approach to this question. The thing that I would probably drill down on is there is a lot of discussion at the moment around CVE.

I have always viewed that, and we have a lot of experience with this in the United Kingdom, is something that I understand why people have to try and why government has to try to take that preventative approach. I don't have massive amounts of confidence in the program as it currently exists, and I do think there are an awful lot of improvements to be made.

But even with improvements, that kind of program, I think is a, it needs to be in the toolbox for all the things you would bring to the counterterrorism, counter-radicalization discussion, but I wouldn't put huge amounts of faith in it.

Ms. JACKSON LEE. I would like Dr. Clarke to be able to answer, Mr. Chairman, and then I would like, Dr. Clarke, if you could comment on the importance of countering violent extremism as a component of our fight?

Mr. CLARKE. Yes. I mean, I pretty much agree with Robin there. I think CVE is important, but I think the literature, the academic literature and I tend to base my judgments off of empirical evidence and data, is so nascent that we really don't know what works and what doesn't.

You know, people are coming out of the woodworks now promising CVE programs as if they were some kind of magic bullet or silver bullet. I just, you know, I totally dismiss that. I think it is important to learn what works and what doesn't, but we are just not there yet.

That doesn't mean throw the baby out with the bath water. It means, you know, buckling down and getting some really smart people to start thinking about this in a focused manner. So and again, it is one pillar in an otherwise broad, comprehensive counterterror strategy.

Ms. JACKSON LEE. OK. Thank you.

Mr. GALLAGHER. Thank you.

Ms. JACKSON LEE. I yield back. Thank you.

Mr. GALLAGHER. The Chair now recognizes the gentleman from Pennsylvania, Mr. Fitzpatrick for 3 minutes.

Mr. FITZPATRICK. Thank you, Mr. Chairman.

Thank you all for being here. I will just address the question to the entire panel. It is the same question I asked Secretary Kelly when he appeared before us regarding Visa Waiver.

So we all know the threats of entry through various mechanisms, whether it be the Northern Border, the Southern Border, the refugee program, the legal immigration process, as was the case with Malik regarding San Bernardino. But I want to address the Visa Waiver Program for a second to the extent that any of you have researched or put some thought into that.

Thirty-eight countries roughly, part of the program started in the 1980's based on the Human Development Index, which is basically higher-income countries. That was the old model back then.

We live in a very different world in 2017 than existed back in the 1980's. The threats have changed, and terrorism is no longer a regional threat.

It is a global threat, and there are a lot of really dangerous people that live in really nice places like Copenhagen and Brussels and Paris and London. There are some really good people that live in really tough places.

The Visa Waiver Program I think last year about 70,000 came in. Currently I think there are about 150,000 overstays. It is I believe a dangerous situation we are in right now when you have a lot of people that have been radicalized in Western Europe that can essentially come in through the waiver process that goes unchecked.

With all the billions of dollars we spend on National security, that seems to be a glaring gap. So I just wanted your perspective on that.

Mr. SIMCOX. Congressman, I know I have colleagues at the Heritage Foundation who have done an awful lot of work on the Visa Waiver Program and are currently supportive of it, although they recognize some of the threats that you outlined.

I would like to be able to give you a fuller answer with a testimony if that is OK?

Mr. JOSCELYN. Just real quick, there are many reasons why I don't think the travel ban, for example, works and is effective at all. This is one of them. So if you look in European nations in terms of how they say the arrests or threats have manifested there, in 2016 Europol says there were 718 jihadist terrorist arrests across the European countries, many of whom, obviously, have a visa waiver in effect.

Only 22 of those arrests were returnees from Iraq and Syria. And 77 of the 718 were returnees from any battlefield, so Iraq, Syria, elsewhere.

So 718 means that basically most of the threats that they are dealing with in Europe who are, can more easily get in to the United States via the Visa Waiver Program from European countries are actually already residents or citizens in Europe.

I think that that—basically that doesn't even—although 718 are potentially going to do that, all I am saying is that if I were looking to plan something in the United States and I wanted to get somebody to go do it, I would use somebody who could get in that way because it is easier.

Mr. FITZPATRICK. Mr. Joscelyn, could you provide the committee with that information when you get it?

Mr. JOSCELYN. Sure. It is actually there. It is in my written testimony, but I can provide more on that one.

Mr. FITZPATRICK. OK.

Mr. CLARKE. I would just add to what Tom said. We are talking about those arrests, and correct me if I am wrong, but those are people that didn't travel to Iraq and Syria. So those are Europeans that never left.

Dan Byman had a piece in Lawfare, either today or yesterday, talking about frustrated foreign fighters. So in some sense it is countries can be a victim of their own success.

We spend a lot of time preventing people from going, right? But now they are home and they are still intent to attack or travel elsewhere to places including the United States to launch an attack.

If I can just quickly, one thing we know about terrorist organizations is that they are highly adaptable. The Islamic State in particular has found a way around sending people from one battlefield to the other.

That is, as I am sure all of you know, the virtual entrepreneur model where they are using encrypted comms to get in touch with people that never left the place to actually direct them through every step of how to conduct an attack. Daveed Gartenstein-Ross and others have written about this extensively.

Mr. FITZPATRICK. I yield back.

Mr. GALLAGHER. Thank you.

The Chair now recognizes the gentleman from Virginia, Mr. Garrett for 3 minutes.

Mr. GARRETT. So I would thank the Chair and Mr. Clarke for providing a wonderful segue into the line of questioning that I have. I was a moderately decent soldier and a competent prosecutor, and I am familiar with 18 Code U.S. 2332(b), which makes illegal acts of terrorism transcending national boundaries and the concepts of conspiracy and intent, which would allow the prosecution of individuals who might not have completed efforts to do these things.

Mr. Joscelyn spoke earlier of an individual in Cleveland who had returned after having been involved with al-Qaeda, and Mr. Clarke talks about individuals from other areas as well.

I have read stories obviously of individuals from the United States who were arrested as they sought to travel to join ISIS. What I have not read is the proactive arrest of individuals who had been identified when they returned.

Mr. Simcox, do you know of any instances where we have identified individuals who have traveled abroad to engage in or support terrorist organizations being arrested upon their return to the United States?

Mr. SIMCOX. Well, the United States I am less familiar with. Europe is—many of those arrests have taken place, but there has been great difficulty in translating evidence or intelligence from the battlefield into courtrooms. So there has not been the success rate with convictions that European governments would have liked.

Mr. GARRETT. Does anyone in the panel, and this is open-ended, familiar with any sort of proactive reverse investigative techniques? For example, we worked hard in a past life on those who might seek to use electronic communication devices to exploit children by creating individuals on-line who might appear to be someone who they are not, for example, a 13-year-old girl who is actually a 34-year-old detective.

Do we ever engage in essentially chatroom conversation with folks who would allege that they had traveled abroad? Does anybody know about anything like that? If so, can you think of a good reason why or why not we might seek to do that sort of thing?

Mr. Joscelyn.

Mr. JOSCELYN. Yes. So one of the things we track and what we journal is the FBI's filings from the different cases. You can see in those filings that they have undercover operatives communicating with people who travel abroad or people who are suspected of being radicalized inside the United States who may commit an attack.

The FBI clearly, if you just go through the filings, it is obvious to me they have a program to basically interdict or sort-of go after people who——

Mr. GARRETT. Sure, and with all due respect, I have got 45 seconds. That makes me feel good and I would argue——

Mr. JOSCELYN. Sure.

Mr. GARRETT [continuing]. Though I would submit that perhaps the recent arrests at Schofield Barracks in Hawaii is indicative of this sort of engagement.

But what I would like to know is given the fact that whether it is a local national, a U.S. citizen, or a foreign national coming to the United States, based on the current code of the United States, specifically 18 U.S. Code 2332, whether the current administration or the previous administration has done anything to round up folks who left the fight and came back?

Because you give me the facts, and I will lock them up. Are we doing that? Anybody?

Mr. Joscelyn.

Mr. JOSCELYN. As the way you stated it probably not, no. We are not doing that, no.

Mr. GARRETT. But you would concede it is illegal to do that, and the statute of limitations is 8 years, why aren't we?

Mr. JOSCELYN. Yes. I mean, the FBI knows—I am not defending the FBI here, but I know the FBI does investigate these people or tries to anyway, on a regular basis.

Now, that doesn't mean they are rounding up and arresting them like you are saying, but they are investigating and trying to stop people that they think or suspect are going to basically pop off.

Mr. GARRETT. Mr. Chairman, I am 11 seconds over. I would submit that if we have laws on the books to arrest and incarcerate individuals who have traveled abroad to engage in and support terrorism and we are not doing it, somebody needs to whisper in the administration's ear. Thank you.

Mr. GALLAGHER. Thank you.

We will now entertain a second round of questions, and I will recognize myself for 3 minutes.

Mr. Simcox, I think you suggested there are 500 French children in Syria, 150 of which have been born in Syria, some 80 Dutch.

Then Mr. Joscelyn, in your written testimony you talk about this cubs of the caliphate program. Talk to us just both of you, just talk a little bit more about that phenomenon and what unique challenges it might pose to our efforts as a task force? Because I think it is an underappreciated phenomenon right now.

Mr. SIMCOX. Well, yes. So one of the complications right off the bat is the citizenship question of some of these children. Are they French? Are they British? Are they Dutch? Are they French Syrian?

That is the first question that is being posed and obviously what we do with these children when they return to their countries of origin. Are there any kind of de-radicalization programs that we could put them through that we are confident would work? I don't think there is.

So in terms of this task force, this is a problem for 10, 20, 30 years down the line where you have these children that have been, I think, brainwashed essentially with violent ideology who will have every right to return to Europe and somewhere down the line every right to travel to the United States. I think we need to be very, very wary of that as a potential future threat.

Mr. JOSCELYN. Just so real quick, one of the more disturbing videos I have seen of late of the many disturbing videos we have seen come out of ISIS will star foreign children who were forced to commit beheadings of men who were imprisoned. They were dressed up like the perpetrators of the November 2015 Paris attacks.

So what happened is before November 2015, some of the men who went off to commit that attack actually committed these brutal executions overseas in Iraq and Syria. These four children reenacted that scene on behalf of ISIS. ISIS made them do that.

The message in the video was very explicit. You are getting some of our guys now. We are raising a new generation to come after you in the future. That was the whole idea and why they were dressed up like the Paris attackers.

This is a massive psychological and security problem for the near future, mainly in Iraq and Syria, but of course elsewhere. This cubs of the caliphate program exists elsewhere. We have seen it in Afghanistan. We have seen it in North Africa.

This is absolutely a form of brainwashing. Back in the communist days in Maoist China and sort-of thing, we have read up on this, one of the reasons they do this is they want to shock the conscience of the person to think there is no way of coming back.

That basically if you commit an absolutely horrific crime, that basically just violates all laws of human nature, then basically there is no way to come back from that. You are then indoctrinated for life.

That is the idea behind it. That is part of what they are trying to do. This creates a massive problem, and I am not going to pretend I have the answers.

Mr. GALLAGHER. Then, I mean, as we look at the audience here today, we have mostly young people that are presumably interested in counterterrorism and National security. I mean, are we on the flip side—and I am going to go over my time, but that is OK.

Are we—that is right. Thank you. Do you think are we doing enough to get that next generation engaged and just recruit the best linguists, regional experts?

Does our security clearance process hinder the recruitment of the best analysts and that sort-of next generation of intelligence professionals and political warriors, if you will, although we have sort-of lost the art of political warfare?

Dr. Clarke, I am interested in your thoughts on that.

Mr. CLARKE. Yes. So maybe I am a bit of an optimist here and in addition to being a political scientist at the RAND Corporation, I am a college professor at Carnegie Mellon University in Pittsburgh, Pennsylvania.

At CMU in particular I was growing a program called the Institute for Politics and Strategy, which is really cross-cutting. It involves people that are involved in cybersecurity.

As you probably know, CMU is a big engineering and computer science school, and so at least from my perch I think there is a lot of interest from younger generations in combining international relations with cybersecurity, which is a huge need, a growing need for our country with some of these other things like robotics, which could be used for the military in the future.

Mr. GALLAGHER. We are out of time, but if there are any recommendations from FDD or Heritage on that front, I think we would welcome them.

The Chair now recognizes the Ranking Member, Mrs. Watson Coleman for 3 minutes.

Mrs. WATSON COLEMAN. Thank you, Mr. Chairman. Thank you for all of your testimony. It has been very interesting and very illuminating. I want to kind of take us back a little bit here.

This task force is to deny foreign fighters entry into the United States of America. So I need to know from you a couple of things, if you don't mind? Is the threat of those folks coming to the United States of America low, medium, or high?

What is it that you think we should do differently than we do now in terms of who comes into this country? Get you to respond to that and whether or not you think that that is our biggest threat or should we be focusing on those who get radicalized here and never leave here but become a threat to us?

So would you all three have at it for me? Thank you.

Mr. JOSCELYN. Just very quickly, what I would say about this is as our security systems are overwhelmed by domestic threats, both in Europe and here in the United States, what I would say is it is a low-probability event that a highly-trained team of foreign fighters could come in here, but I think there is a higher probability to it than it is ascribed in the bureaucracy, is the way I would put it.

So we have to be very careful because what is happening now with the FBI and the other security services is they are being overwhelmed by, you know, the 18-year-old who is downloading an ISIS magazine in their parents' basement in Staten Island, OK?

That guy may be a threat, but it does not necessarily deserve the amount of resources that he is being given. This is part of the conversations I am having is sort-of I think there is a resource allocation problem that is potentially could be exposed here by our enemies. I will leave it at that.

Mr. SIMCOX. I would just add that I think that in terms of the plots, the most numerous are probably from the home-grown radicals that never made the trip to Syria or Iraq. But in terms of the potential scale of carnage, I would say the highest threat comes from those who have traveled to those conflict zones, fought and trained with these terrorist groups and come back and try and carry out an attack.

I mean, just look at what happened in Paris. I think the highest risk in terms of the body count, to be frank, comes from that kind of fighter.

Mrs. WATSON COLEMAN. I am interested in knowing the level of threat you think it is to our homeland: Low, medium, or high? I understand what you are saying.

Mr. CLARKE. I would say I agree with Tom. I think it is a low-probability, high-impact event though. So we talk all the time about black swans, the unknowable event that has a catastrophic impact.

I think this is probably more along the lines of a gray swan, something that is imminently knowable but we also have to do the legwork, connect the dots and share intelligence and work with our partners overseas to put those pieces together.

It is not a fait accompli that we will just figure this out because we put a lot of resources into intel. We also have to do the hard work to get there.

Mr. GALLAGHER. The Chair now recognizes the gentleman from Virginia, Mr. Garrett for 3 minutes.

Mr. GARRETT. So we have three intelligent people in front of this committee, Mr. Chair, or this subcommittee. Along the line of questioning I touched on earlier is Sweden recently made it a crime to travel to engage in terrorist activity and support.

You talked earlier, I believe Mr. Simcox, about encouraging Europeans to, and I quote, which is frightening, "to spend money and to take this seriously." If the person with terminal lung cancer won't quit smoking it is hard to help them.

But I would open the floor and we will go Joscelyn, Simcox, and Clarke in order. I have got about 2 minutes, to you gentlemen to suggest actions that would be appropriately within the purview of the Legislative branch of the U.S. Federal Government that might further the goal of making our homeland safer from returning would-be jihadists, radicals, or anything tangentially related thereto?

We don't have a monopoly on good ideas. What are we not doing that you think we might do more of within the purview of this body?

Mr. JOSCELYN. I have to review the laws. I am not sure what you—I think you hinted at basically something that was not being enforced basically on the legal side. I have to look into that a little bit more.

If our current material support for terrorism laws are not being fully sort-of leveraged to the extent that they could be, that may be—I don't know if that is something that could be encouraged from this body or not. But that is something to look at.

I think that there was a sort-of a lag during the Obama administration on the full sort-of implementation of material support for terrorism laws, and I would look into that is what I would say.

Mr. GARRETT. Thank you very much. I will tell you that we looked at carrying a bill to do what Sweden did realized we had laws on the books that could deal with that, but that they need to be uniformly enforced. On the answers to the questions I asked you earlier are, yes, we do that sometimes.

But to the best of my ability to ascertain, no we don't do it all the time, and I can't figure out why not.

Mr. Simcox, what should we be doing differently within the purview of the Legislative branch?

Mr. SIMCOX. There is a clear need here to take on the ideology in a way that I don't think was done over the last 8 years. There was a lot of talking around the problem.

I think that taking the European approach that the language around CVE, the community-led approach, I understand the arguments behind there. I don't think there is any great success that it has worked, either in the United States or in any European country. So I would suggest we need to re-look at that.

Mr. GARRETT. Thank you.

Dr. Clarke.

Mr. CLARKE. So I think before we jump to enact any kind of legislation we need to figure out what works and what doesn't.

Mr. GARRETT. Sure.

Mr. CLARKE. I am referring here specifically to the use of social media. So there was a big announcement a couple of weeks ago about some of the tech giants, Facebook and others, that they are becoming more active in shutting down websites and trying to discard jihadist ideology.

I am just not sure, not because I think it is a bad idea, but I genuinely don't know if it is better to shut down the websites or to keep them up and running just to monitor them.

Mr. GARRETT. Dr. Clarke, I think you made an amazing point. I also think that when we start determining what speech isn't acceptable it is a very slippery slope.

I do wish, however, we would do a better job of differentiating how we treat American citizens and foreign nationals because the bountiful blessings bestowed upon us by our Constitution and Bill of Rights, in my estimation, don't extend to those who come here to do us harm from abroad.

Mr. CLARKE. But I see it as a form of open-source intelligence——

Mr. GARRETT. Yes, I agree.

Mr. CLARKE [continuing]. And open-source networks.

Mr. GARRETT. Thank you. Thank you.

Thank you, Mr. Chair.

Mr. GARRETT. The Chair now recognizes the gentlelady from Texas, Ms. Jackson Lee for 3 minutes.

Ms. JACKSON LEE. Thank you very much. I want to pursue Dr. Clarke's thought of open-source and form of securing, soliciting, or obtaining better intelligence. But let me indicate that, or at least pose a question, about the weaponizing of cyber and that that now adds a different component to whether it is a returning fighter, whether it is somebody on social media.

The question I asked you all originally was the assessment of how we should focus our resources, FBI, intelligence resources, et cetera.

Let me be very clear. A lot of resources are now being used to follow the tracks of the Russian connection, the Russian collusion, children of Donald Trump having conversations with known affiliates of the Kremlin.

Having just come back from a former Soviet Bloc country, Belarus, there is no doubt that every effort that the Russian and Russian affiliates have to follow, track, undermine the United States they will do it. Their leader is a KGB.

So the issue becomes the choice and use of resources. So terrorism is defined as somebody else's flower, somebody else's terrorism. The question becomes how do we allocate the resources?

Do you consider the need for us to be able to follow both streams of potential threat to the United States and using heavy resources in both categories following the Russian intrusion, the election, collusion with the election, trying to recruit or penetrating individuals that are close to the White House?

Then, of course, the idea of a different component, a returning fighter or someone, if you will, becoming radicalized on the social network?

Dr. Clarke.

Mr. CLARKE. So let me say I am here as a subject-matter expert on terrorism, but to put on my international security hat for a second, I don't view these as different things.

I view—to use kind-of Pentagon parlance the four-plus-one threat, so both nation-states and violent non-state actors as part of the suite or portfolio of threats that the United States faces. So I don't think that we get to choose who we get to defend against and who we don't.

I think we need to take a broad approach to countering all of our enemies and we are also moving into places like the gray zone and hybrid warfare. So again, it would be nice to pick and choose what we could react to, but again, we have got to do it all.

Ms. JACKSON LEE. Anyone else?

Mr. JOSCELYN. I will just say this on Russia. They are prolific at hybrid warfare and information warfare and cyber intrusions and all of these things.

We absolutely need to devote resources across the board to figuring out exactly what they have tried to do here in the United States and what they are trying to do to Western democracies writ large, because this is a sustained effort by Russia. It is not a one-off type of event.

Mr. SIMCOX. Very quickly on the counterterrorism side of things, there was a period maybe a year, 18 months ago when an awful lot of attention was paid to the social media side of things.

I think the social media side of things is important when it comes to recruitment, but I still think that the key to this is face-to-face individual contacts with people who know each other and draw people into terrorist networks that way. On-line is important, but it is not the whole ball game.

Ms. JACKSON LEE. Well, let me just finish this point, Mr. Chairman. Thank you for your indulgence. I agree with all three of you, and I guess that is the point that I am making is that we need to have pointed resources, Dr. Clarke, that doesn't leave any aspect that may be a threat to the United States.

I will just cite—I am on the Judiciary Committee—the Department of Justice had grants that were going to educate local law enforcement to be—not a little bit, but to be sophisticated in fettering out these individuals who may be in the community or also being able to intervene.

I think that is an element that is equally important because now who is going to catch them at the border's edge on our border, and if they are radicalized here we need to have local communities being a little bit more informed.

But my final point is, it is a multi-task situation, and I hope that that is something we get out of this task force that we need to be looking at a Russia. We need to be looking at those who may potentially come from the fight, start the fight here, because our idea is to protect the homeland.

With that, I yield back. Thank you all for your testimony.

Mr. GALLAGHER. Thank you. I would love to continue questioning, but—well, since Mr. Joscelyn self-identified as a nerd I would love to continue nerding out with all of you on this topic. But we have kept you here 2 hours longer than we anticipated, and we want to be respectful of your time and everyone else's time.

I thank you very much for your flexibility, your patience, and for your thoughtful testimony. I know you spend an enormous amount of time sitting in tanks and thinking and would love nothing more than your thoughts to become legislative reality or policy that is implemented.

I just would submit that you have an opportunity to do just that, and I would hope that the three of you will continue to work with this task force as we go forward.

We welcome all of the ideas you have as we draft our report and as we continue to study this issue. We are trying to recommend concrete things that our Government can do to do a better job of keeping terrorists out of this country, a very complex topic, one that you have all suggested we are going to be dealing with for years to come.

There are no silver bullet solutions, but we are asking you for your best ideas. So please, I just would ask for you to continue working with us and the staff here on that.

I want to thank the Ranking Member for her help and support. I want to thank everyone who showed up for this important hearing. I want to thank all of the young people that attended this. This is an important topic, and I hope you will pursue a career in this field. We need you.

So with that, pursuant to committee Rule VII(D), the hearing record will be held open for 10 days. Without objection, the task force stands adjourned.

[Whereupon, at 4:33 p.m., the task force was adjourned.]

APPENDIX

QUESTIONS FROM CHAIRMAN MIKE GALLAGHER FOR THOMAS JOSCELYN

Question 1. You described the process of terrorists returning from the battlefield to Europe. How, practically speaking, would terrorists find the money to support this travel? Are they still able to find the funds in light of the loss of territorial control?

Answer. Response was not received at the time of publication.

Question 2. In light of the tighter border security between Turkey and the European Union, how would the foreign fighters book flights to return to Europe or other locations? How might they go about falsifying their identities?

Answer. Response was not received at the time of publication.

Question 3. Experts have articulated that as ISIS continues to lose territory, some foreign fighters may seek out other terrorist organizations. What other conflict zones may these fighters flock to and how will these foreign fighters interact with other terrorist organizations such as al-Qaeda? Is it likely they will be absorbed by these other terror groups or will they remain a distinct organization?

Answer. Response was not received at the time of publication.

QUESTIONS FROM CHAIRMAN MIKE GALLAGHER FOR ROBIN SIMCOX

Question 1. As you mentioned in your testimony, entire families have moved to Iraq and Syria and many children have been born in the caliphate. There is concern that ISIS has been training minors in Iraq and Syria to be "the next generation of foreign terrorist fighters," and it is likely that those with Western parents will eventually return home. How can Europe protect itself against this threat, which may not manifest itself for several years?

Answer. Governments cannot be complacent about the threat that radicalized teenagers and pre-teens can pose. Teens or pre-teens featured in almost a quarter of plots in Europe between January 2014 and May 2017.

As children return from the "Caliphate" back to Europe, there is unlikely to be a fool-proof approach which European governments will be able to adopt to protect themselves. However, some steps can be taken.

Clearly, intelligence agencies need to be cognizant of the potential threat that these children could pose in the short, medium, and long term, and work closely with law enforcement when appropriate.

However, a thorough psychological assessment of these children is also necessary, with child protection agencies and social workers engaged. Parents should lose custody rights to their children in some circumstances.

Education is also important. Teachers, for example, could be trained to be aware of the potential signs of radicalization in their students. In the United Kingdom, legislation has been passed—as part of the U.K.'s broader Preventing Violent Extremism (PVE) strategy—to ensure that teachers are required to be on the lookout for this as part of their broader safeguarding duty, much as they would to try and ensure children were not becoming involved with gangs, drugs, or being sexually exploited.

Ultimately, however, this is a generational problem. As long as the ideology of Islamism exists, there lies the possibility of even children being drawn into terrorism and extremism.

Question 2. The United Kingdom's impending exit from the European Union will certainly have enormous ramifications. In the security sphere, how do you think Brexit will affect information sharing and cooperation between the United Kingdom and the European Union, especially with regard to Europol and the Schengen Information System? What impact will Brexit have, if any, on the U.S.-U.K. security and information-sharing relationship?

Answer. The United Kingdom has a series of bilateral intelligence-sharing relationships, which should be unaffected by Brexit. The intelligence-sharing relationship with the United States—and the rest of the Five Eyes community—was extraordinarily robust before Brexit and will continue to be so afterwards.

Countries within the European Union are aware of the United Kingdom's vast intelligence-gathering capacity. It is, therefore, very much in the interest of the United Kingdom's friends in the European Union for cooperation to continue.

One example of where cooperation will likely continue is over the Schengen Information System (SIS). The United Kingdom currently submits information to the SIS. The European Union cutting off the United Kingdom's access to it benefits no one and can only harm collective European security. Furthermore, a non-E.U. country having some form of access to the SIS is not an unprecedented situation (Iceland, for example).

When it comes to Europol, the United Kingdom has never relied on this body as much as some other European countries do. Still, the influence Britain has to shape European Union bodies such as Europol will likely diminish with Brexit.

However, it is not yet clear whether the United Kingdom has to leave Europol entirely. Europol has a variety of organizational agreements with countries outside the European Union and the United Kingdom could potentially arrange a similar agreement.

It is also important not to overstate Europol's efficacy. It is a place for information sharing on a variety of law enforcement issues and focused on improving coordination and cooperation within the European Union. Yet Europol has no power of arrest and can only ever be as powerful as the nations involved will allow it to be. If they are not sharing intelligence with Europol—and that has proven to be the case consistently—then Europol's usefulness as an intelligence-sharing hub is clearly limited anyway.

Question 3. The American NCTC brings together the intelligence community and law enforcement in a way that allows both branches to cooperate in identifying and interdicting terrorists. To what extent has Europe had success or faced challenges in facilitating the flow of information between law enforcement and intelligence?

Answer. Ensuring that information is going back and forth between intelligence and law enforcement agencies is an on-going challenge for many countries in Europe, although European officials state that progress has been made, particularly since ISIS' attack in Brussels in March 2016.

According to a BBC analysis, there are occasions when, "for a Belgian police officer to find out what Belgian intelligence knows about a threat, he or she sometimes needs to learn it from the U.K. police, who learn it from U.K. intelligence, who learn it from Belgian intelligence." These turf wars doubtless limit the operational effectiveness of many European countries' efforts.

There are a multitude of reasons behind this. If a European spy agency is handed intelligence from a foreign country, it may be that it is shared under the agreement that this intelligence is then not passed on to others. This secrecy is understandable. Revealing intelligence haphazardly can lead to the compromising of sources, potentially endangering agents in the field and national security more broadly.

The structure of European countries also presents a problem. Belgium, for example, has very localized policing arrangements: There are six separate police forces just in Brussels. Another example is Germany, whose Federal structure makes it harder to centralize intelligence.

At other times, a country's particular history is a hindrance. Conversations with German officials have demonstrated that the country remains highly resistant to further integration of police and intelligence agencies due to memories of the Gestapo.

Question 4. What progress has Europe made on the judicial front in prosecuting cases of terrorism or material support?

Answer. European countries have had success with prosecuting Islamist terrorists. In the United Kingdom, for example, a Henry Jackson Society report has shown that there were 264 convictions for Islamism-inspired terrorism offences as a result of arrests taking place between 1998 and 2015.

However, issues remain. European countries have found it easier to prosecute those planning attacks than those verbally encouraging or inciting such attacks, or voicing support for terrorist groups. This is partially because freedom of speech issues come into play, but also because legislation may not always be robust enough to be able to sustain successful prosecutions.

Those who have fought in Syria and then return to their countries of origin are also not always easy to prosecute. For a multitude of reasons, it is very hard for European police forces to travel to Syria to collate evidence from a war zone and then use that evidence in a civilian court. The reality is that European governments will not be able to prosecute anything like all returning fighters from the Syria/Iraq conflict. This is not something unique to the war in Syria. Over the past 25 years, thousands of Europeans have traveled to fight in Afghanistan, Bosnia, Iraq, Kashmir, Somalia, and Yemen without prosecution.

Convictions are only part of the solution anyway as long as there is a relaxed approach to sentencing and law and order more generally. Take the example of Ibrahim el-Bakraoui. As part of an armed robbery he was taking part in Brussels, he shot a police officer with a Kalashnikov. El-Bakraoui was sentenced to 9 years in prison in August 2010. However, by 2014, he had been released. This release was sanctioned under the condition that he did not leave Belgium for any longer than a month at a time. El-Bakraoui ignored this, and in June 2015, was thwarted in his attempt to enter Syria, being detained in Turkey and sent back to Europe. Despite this, el-Bakraoui remained free to be part of the ISIS cell that carried out attacks in Brussels in March 2016, killing 32 and injuring approximately 300.

QUESTIONS FROM CHAIRMAN MIKE GALLAGHER FOR COLIN P. CLARKE

Question 1. You've described the Islamic State of Iraq and Syria (ISIS) as a global group that is regionally anchored and sees its members as players in local conflicts. When it comes to Europe, what is the ISIS strategy? Are they hiding in place or is the problem less severe than that? What about the United States? Are they hoping to attack the United States directly or through proxies? What is their long-term goal when it comes to both the United States and Europe?

Answer. In terms of what the ISIS strategy is in Europe, I'd say that it is multitiered. First, I expect ISIS to continue to use its propaganda to attempt to radicalize people living in Europe in hopes of convincing them to launch terrorist attacks, what we might call the classic "lone-wolf" or inspired terrorist. Second, ISIS will attempt to make direct contact with individuals through the internet in what many have called the "virtual planning model" of terrorist attacks, in which ISIS members direct the individuals through encrypted applications and help them plan each step of the attack. Third, it is likely that ISIS members are in Europe, either with or without direct instructions, and these members or cells could conduct attacks similar in style to the November 2015 attacks in Paris. Fourth, and finally, ISIS will likely continue to send fighters from the Middle East to try to surreptitiously infiltrate Europe to conduct attacks.

The situation for the United States is different, because the United States is insulated by two oceans and thus safer as a matter of pure geography. The United States also benefits from more-robust defenses, including superior security and intelligence services and far fewer overall targets. Furthermore, it appears that U.S. policing, intelligence, and border officials have been able to prevent ISIS members from arriving in the United States, although there is no way to be certain of this. ISIS will likely focus its attempts on the first two options listed above (lone-wolf and virtual planning model) but might also attempt something similar to the recent plot in Australia, in which ISIS mailed explosives to terrorists already living in the country. There is a lower probability (albeit not a negligible one) that ISIS will attempt to send fighters directly to the United States via air travel from Europe or the Middle East, or first to Canada and Mexico or points south and then over the border into the United States.

ISIS' long-term goal when it comes to the United States and Europe is to continue sowing terror and trying to show U.S. and European citizens that their governments are incapable of protecting them. Most experts assess that ISIS would ideally like to conduct an attack in a U.S. or European city using chemical weapons. ISIS, like al-Qaeda, also remains fixated on attacking aviation, as evidenced by the recent plot in Australia.

Question 2. The recent pace of terrorist plots and attacks in Europe, carried out by both home-grown extremists and foreign fighter returnees, has been staggering. Since the rise of ISIS, the West has experience several "lone-wolf" attacks, where the attackers were seemingly inspired by ISIS' ideology or carried the attack out in the name of ISIS. Is it accurate to describe these attacks as "lone wolves," or after closer examination, do ISIS members usually play some role in facilitating the attacks? How should the West address the threat of ISIS operatives exploiting ungoverned spaces to continue directly or indirectly executing and inspiring attacks?

Answer. ISIS operatives do not follow one simple model in planning terrorist attacks; instead, the operatives hedge their bets to achieve the highest rate of success in conducting an attack. There have indeed been true lone wolves who have merely been inspired by Salafi-jihadist ideology—the ISIS and al-Qaeda ideology that seeks to emulate the presumed practices of the earliest generation of Muslims and that believes in violent struggle against non-Muslims and apostates as an important religious duty. But ISIS would prefer to play a more direct role in these attacks, because virtual planner-style attacks or ISIS-directed attacks involving trained militants dispatched to attack a target typically result in higher lethality rates.

With respect to ungoverned spaces, I think the term itself is somewhat misleading. ISIS prefers "alternatively governed" spaces, where the government in place is tribal, clan-based, or generally anti-Western and that either is overtly tolerant of extremists operating from its soil or lacks the capacity to do anything about it. In the West, I'm very concerned about places like Molenbeek, Belgium, and the banlieues of France, the ex-urban, depressed suburbs that are homes to many immigrants and that have seemingly become incubators of extremism and given rise to hundreds of jihadists determined to attack the West. In these cases, Western governments need to devise a plan to root out extremists, which is not only a multi-generational effort but one comprising economic, political, social, cultural, religious, and security dimensions. Finally, it will be crucial to monitor social media and online activity to ensure that ISIS does not find safe haven in the virtual space.

○